3381

KU-774-806

INTELLIGENCE AND
ATTAINMENT TESTS

INTELLIGENCE AND ATTAINMENT TESTS

P. E. VERNON

Professor of Educational Psychology,
University of London, Institute of Education

UNIVERSITY OF LONDON PRESS LTD
WARWICK SQUARE, LONDON E.C.4

Copyright © 1960
by P. E. Vernon
Reprinted 1961

Printed & Bound in England for the UNIVERSITY OF LONDON PRESS LTD.,
by HAZELL WATSON & VINEY LTD., Aylesbury and Slough

CONTENTS

PREFACE

DESPITE all the work that has been done by British psychologists in the field of mental testing, it is curious that no textbook has been published since Ballard's pioneering volumes in the early twenties. There are many useful but brief accounts, both in books for teachers and for psychology students, but these do not attempt to cover all the main tests in common use, and they seldom bring out the underlying principles of test construction or of the interpretation of test results. There are also admirable full-scale books by American authors. However, these represent a rather different attitude to testing and its uses from that current here; and they cover far too many tests which have no relevance for us.

I have tried therefore to supply a book which will meet the needs of students of psychology, while at the same time making it sufficiently simple to be useful to teachers or others interested in education, the social sciences, or generally in assessing, selecting, or guiding human beings. I have also referred to British research literature, where available, rather than to American, since the latter has often been ably summarised elsewhere.

A further reason for writing this book is that the views of psychologists on the nature of intelligence, and on what intelligence tests measure, have become modified considerably over the past third of a century. There is much that is controversial in this field; hence my aim has been to give a balanced view, and to show how this is supported by the experimental evidence. If, as I shall conclude, the intelligence we are measuring is not primarily an innate capacity, a good deal of reorientation is required in our views on the uses to be made of tests.

I am indebted to several colleagues for reading and criticising the manuscript, notably Dr. C. A. Rogers of the University of Southern Rhodesia, Dr. D. M. Lee and Dr. W. H. King of the

London Institute of Education, and my sister, Professor M. D. Vernon. Acknowledgments are also made to the following for permission to reproduce tables or other material: Mr. J. C. Raven (Fig. 7), Houghton, Mifflin Co. (Table VI), Stanford University Press (Table XI), and the Controller of H.M. Stationery Office (Table X).

January, 1959   P. E. VERNON

Chapter One

HISTORICAL INTRODUCTION

THE Press, together with most members of the British public, still seem to regard intelligence tests and tests of educational attainments with a good deal of suspicion. They are thought of as something new-fangled, invented by psychologists, and as much less trustworthy or well-tried than the ordinary school examination. In fact their history goes back fifty years or more; as early as 1920 they were fully developed, were being applied to most of their present-day purposes, and had been shown to be superior to examinations for many such purposes. Many of the criticisms and suspicions that one still hears, then, are based on misunderstandings, which it is the object of this book to dispel. At the same time these tests *are* open to various imperfections and difficulties; and these too we will try to describe impartially.

In the latter half of the nineteenth century, the early psychologists devoted considerable attention to the measurement of sensory capacities. For example, they tested the smallest difference in the pitch of sounds, or in the heaving of weights, that people could detect. Also they studied reaction time, or quickness of response, mechanical memorising, and other rather elementary abilities. It was soon found, however, that such abilities bore little relation to the intelligence of students or to their educational achievements. The first test of higher intellectual abilities was devised by Ebbinghaus in 1897, and known as the Completion Test. This tried to show a child's capacity to comprehend and relate ideas by getting him to fill in missing words in a story:

Ex. 1. One ( ) ( ) eagle (   ) with the ( ) birds ( ) see (   )
       day the   went   other   to   which

could ( ) ( ) highest. . . .
     fly the

However, it was the French psychologist, Alfred Binet, who first arrived at the essential principles of mental testing and who produced, in 1905, the first practicable scale for expressing intelligence in numerical units.

THE BINET-SIMON SCALES

For many years Binet had studied the physical and mental development of his own daughters, and had noted their growth, from year to year, in comprehending, reasoning, judgment, and other intellectual capacities. Thus when he was approached by the Paris education authorities with a request for assistance in discovering children who were too dull to be educated in ordinary schools, he conceived the possibility of a series of mental tasks which would be characteristic of the development of normal children of a given age. The average 6-year old, for example, was found to be capable of giving his age, reproducing a sentence of 16 syllables, counting 13 pennies correctly, copying a diamond shape, and defining 'horse', 'chair', etc., in terms of use. But a retarded child might not achieve the same tasks until he was 7, 8 or more, and could thus be said to be one or two years behind in his intellectual development or *Mental Age*. Suppose it was found, for example, that repetition of 16 syllables was done correctly by some 15 per cent of 4-year olds, 40 per cent of 5-year olds, 73 per cent of 6-year olds and 85 per cent of 7-year olds: this task was then assigned to the 6-year level on Binet's scale, and children who passed this and other 6-year items were said to have a Mental Age of 6, although their actual or chronological age might be higher or lower than 6.

Numerous tasks were tried out by Binet and his collaborator, Simon, as providing samples or specimens of children's intellectual development. They were compared also with teachers' judgments of the children's intelligence—in other words, tasks or items were chosen which were passed more frequently by children whom teachers regarded as bright than by those regarded as dull. The original series of items of 1905 was revised in 1908 and 1911. The latter Binet-Simon scale consisted of 55 items, 5 for each age—3, 4, ... 10, 12, 15 years and adult. Translations and adaptations into English were soon made by Goddard in America and Burt in England. Their scales, too, were used primarily for assessing the dull and feeble-minded. But in 1916, L. M. Terman of Stanford University published a more extensive revision which was capable of covering almost the whole range of intelligence from 3-year to adult levels. This Stanford-Binet scale was the most useful, and the most widely applied, of all psychological tests for the next twenty-one years.

Binet had observed that children's responses were somewhat irregular, in that they often failed some items at a lower level than their Mental Age and passed other items at a higher level. Thus a more detailed scoring system was introduced. Suppose the complete record of a 5:0-year old to be:

> 3-year tests 5/5 passed
> 4-year „ 4/5 „
> 5-year „ 2/5 „
> 6-year „ 1/5 „
> 7-year „ 0/5 „

In this case the 3-year level, where all tests are passed, is called the *basal age*. Each subsequent test passed, that is seven in all, gives a credit of one-fifth of a year. So the final Mental Age is $3 + \frac{7}{5} = 4\frac{2}{5}$ years, or approximately 4 years 5 months.

It was also observed that the degree of retardation or advancement, in Mental Age years, tended to increase as children got older. A child who was 1 year backward at 5 would be more likely to be 2 years than 1 year backward at 10. The German psychologist, Stern, suggested that the ratio of Mental to Chronological Age would remain relatively constant, and Terman denoted this *Mental Ratio* (multiplied by 100) as the *Intelligence Quotient* or *I.Q.*

$$I.Q. = \frac{M.A.}{C.A.} \times 100$$

Thus our 5:0-year old with a M.A. of $4\frac{2}{5}$ years has an I.Q. of 88. A child who is just normal for his age has, by definition, an I.Q. of 100. I.Q.s of 130 to 150 or more are regarded as very superior, and those below 70 or so usually indicate feeble-mindedness or mental defect (cf. p. 166). We shall discuss later the extent to which this I.Q. really remains constant as a child grows older.

With the approach of maturity a complication arises. The growth of intelligence seems to slow down soon after 12 years and to cease somewhere around 14 to 16 years (this statement, too, will require later qualifications). Thus the average adult obtains a Binet Mental Age of, say, 15, and if we continued to calculate his I.Q. by the usual formula it would obviously decline progressively,

which is absurd. By the age of 30 it would drop from 100 to 50,
i.e. $\dfrac{15 \times 100}{30}$. To overcome this difficulty, testers often divide
an adult's M.A. by some constant figure, say 15 (or 14 or 16),
instead of by his real age. However, we recognise that the system
of measuring intelligence or other abilities in terms of age-units
has many difficulties, and that it breaks down seriously during
adolescence and adulthood. Some modern tests continue to express
a person's standing in terms of so-called quotients, but—as we
shall see—these are very differently derived (p. 50).

Before leaving this topic, let us be clear regarding the meanings
of M.A. and I.Q. The former, not the latter, represents a child's
present intelligence level. The I.Q. is primarily an index of rate of
intellectual growth, and thus, secondarily, a prediction of his
ultimate level when he has reached maturity on the assumption
that this rate of growth continues. Consider two children, A
and B:

A. C.A. 10:0   M.A. 12:0   I.Q. 120

B. C.A. 11:0   M.A. 12:6   I.Q. 114

B is the more intelligent in the sense of being capable of the more
difficult intellectual work at the moment. A, with the higher
I.Q., is more intelligent only in the sense that he is likely to catch
up with, and eventually to surpass, B. However, in a group of
children all very close together in age (say, a class taking the
11-year selection examinations), either M.A. or I.Q. will give
much the same information about their relative intelligence
levels.[1]

THE WORK OF CHARLES SPEARMAN

In the early days of testing there was much controversy as to
how far people's capacities depend on *general* intelligence, or how
far they are *specific* or distinct. As already mentioned, sensory
discrimination and reaction time seemed to be largely specific.
Binet, however, assumed that the varied tasks which went to make
up his scale were all samples of the same general intellectual
ability. It was the British psychologist, Spearman, who realised

---

[1] The practice of using I.Q.s and Educational Quotients in secondary school
selection, rather than Mental Ages or test scores, is quite sound, since otherwise
the youngest children in a year-group would be unfairly handicapped (cf.
Vernon, 1957: Bibliography).

that questions of this kind could be investigated scientifically by finding the precise amount of correspondence between various abilities.

The statistical work of Sir Francis Galton and Karl Pearson in the nineteenth century had provided an index, known as the *correlation coefficient*, or *r*, for expressing the correspondence between any two sets of measurements of a group of people. This index ranges from +1·0 (perfect agreement), through 0·0 (no agreement either way), to —1·0 (negative or inverse agreement). Thus if a class of children are ranked in order for problem arithmetic and mechanical arithmetic, the correlation between the two orders is likely to be very close—a coefficient of +0·8 or over. But if their arithmetic and handwriting marks are compared, the correlation may be much lower; some good arithmeticians are poor writers, and vice versa. But on the whole those good in one subject are also above average in other subjects, thus the coefficient is likely to be low positive, say +0·30. Arithmetic and age, on the other hand, may yield a negative correlation of —0·2 or lower, when—as often happens—the brightest children in a school class tend to be the youngest.

Now Spearman noted that all tests, even of abilities as diverse as classics, mathematics, musical ability, weight discrimination and teachers' ratings for 'cleverness', correlated positively (though to varying extents), suggesting that there was some underlying general ability running through all of them; and this common element he designated as *g* or the factor of general ability. At the same time, in so far as the correlations were always well below 1·0, he suggested that every ability involves, besides *g*, something specific, which he called an *s*-factor. Thus musical ability and weight discrimination show only a small positive correlation because, while both depend partly on *g*, music also depends on a specific musical capacity and weight discrimination on a quite independent capacity. Spearman's work from 1904 onwards was largely devoted to showing that most of the correlations between tests of different abilities could be accounted for in terms of *g* and *s* factors (the Two-Factor Theory).[1] He found that

---

[1] A particularly clear exposition of the complex arguments and statistical calculations underlying the Two-Factor Theory is given by R. Knight (1943). Spearman's fullest statement of his methods and results is *The Abilities of Man* (1927). Cf. also Vernon (1956) for an elementary, and (1950) for a more advanced treatment.

tests which involved g to the greatest extent were those with the highest intellectual content, for example school marks in classics, or tests of solving analogies or classifying similarities. These, too, tended to correlate most highly with teachers' assessments of their pupils' intelligence. But tests like mechanical arithmetic and sensory discrimination were more highly specific, or less 'g-saturated'. The essence of g appeared to be the capacity for grasping relations or, as Spearman put it, for educing relations and correlates. Thus in the analogy:

Ex. 2. Leg is to Knee as Arm is to . . . ?

the person being tested must first comprehend the relation of *Leg* to *Knee*, and then apply it to the third term, *Arm*, in order to arrive at the answer, *Elbow*.

Spearman did not, in fact, identify g with intelligence, since—as shown in our next chapter—it was almost impossible to arrive at an acceptable definition of what intelligence means. By contrast, g is the highest common factor that can be extracted from any set of tests; it is an objective and mathematically definable quantity. However, his theory provided a basis for the construction of intelligence tests. Since every test has its own s-component, no one test can yield a pure measure of g. But by combining the results from several tests, each one preferably having a high g-saturation, the total score is likely to be almost wholly a measure of g, as the various specific components will tend to cancel one another out. So that although Binet's procedure of throwing together a number of varied items which appeared to him to provide a broad sampling of children's intellectual development was haphazard and unscientific, it was nevertheless likely to yield quite a reliable test of g. Spearman's work, then, has played a fundamental part in the growth of intelligence testing although, as we shall see later, his Two-Factor Theory has by now been abandoned.

THE RISE OF EDUCATIONAL MEASUREMENT

Investigations of school and university examinations from 1888 onwards had shown that the marking is often highly subjective and unreliable. Different markers of the same essays or other papers vary widely in their standards and in the qualities which they regard as desirable or undesirable. However, disagreement is minimised in examinations of certain kinds of attainment such as spelling or simple arithmetic sums, where only one right answer to each question is possible. Around 1908–10, therefore, Thorndike, Courtis and other American educational psychologists prepared tests of these and other subjects, consisting of sets of questions or items which could be scored objectively. Standards or norms of performance were provided by applying them to pupils in a large number of schools. Thus the typical or average performance for third grade, fourth grade, etc., pupils was determined, and any new pupil could be assessed against these standards. Alternatively the scores of successive age-groups were established so that, as in the Binet test, results could be expressed in age units. A bright 9-year old, for example, might do as well as an average 11-year old on an arithmetic test, and thus be said to have an Arithmetic Age of 11. In this way a meaningful and well-defined set of units was substituted for the variable standards of percentage or other marks awarded by teachers and examiners. Educational Quotients, analogous to Intelligence Quotients, could also be calculated.[1]

This approach to educational measurement was soon extended to more complex skills and attainments. Scales were developed for assessing the quality of handwriting, and the new-type or objective examination was put forward to overcome the defects of the conventional essay-type examination. Instead of setting students a few complex questions, their answers to which inevitably led to discrepancies between examiners, each topic was reduced to a number of brief questions so arranged that only one right answer to each was possible. These included:

(i) the simple question or completion form

Ex. 3. What is the capital city of France? . . .

4. Napoleon was finally defeated at the battle of . . . in the year . . .

---

[1] The terms E.Q. and A.Q. are often used to refer to English and Arithmetic Quotients. Sometimes, however, E.Q. means Educational Quotient, representing the child's average performance on a complete set of attainment tests; and A.Q. means Achievement or Accomplishment Quotient, which is derived from $\frac{E.A.}{M.A.}$ or $\frac{E.Q.}{I.Q.}$ (cf. p. 120). To avoid confusion it would be better to call the school subject quotients En.Q. and Ar.Q.

(ii) statements to be marked True or False

> 5. The author of *The Fairie Queene* was Christopher
>   Marlowe   TRUE   FALSE

and (iii) the multiple-choice item, together with various more complex derivatives (cf. Vernon, 1956).

> 6. Sound travels most quickly through:
>   A. cold water
>   B. hot water
>   C. the air
>   D. a vacuum

The new-type form was rapidly adopted in America, not only for standardised educational tests in different school subjects, but also by schools and colleges generally for the majority of their internal examinations. A strong case for its use in England was made by P. B. Ballard in *The New Examiner* (1923), but it never won the same popularity among British educationists, except in standardised tests for educational selection and guidance.

In 1913 Burt was appointed as the first educational psychologist to an education authority, namely the London County Council, and in the ensuing eight years he developed a comprehensive series of educational tests, covering the 5–14 age range, for purposes of individual study of backward children, and for surveying levels of attainment, in different schools or different London boroughs. These were published, together with his adaptation of the Binet-Simon scale, and other contributions to the theory and practice of testing, in *Mental and Scholastic Tests* in 1921.

The results of any one such test can be expressed as a Reading Age, Spelling Age, etc., and by applying a series of tests to the same child, his relative standing in different educational skills can be shown as a graph or profile. For example, his Reading and Composition Ages, like his Mental Age, might be superior to his Chronological Age, but his Arithmetic Age very much lower. No such precise comparisons are possible from ordinary unstandardised school examinations.

GROUP INTELLIGENCE TESTS

It was but a short step from the individually administered Binet test and the printed group test of educational attainment to the group intelligence test. In 1916, A. S. Otis in America was constructing sets of analogies, opposites, and other types of items involving intellectual comprehension. Each set contained questions ranging from easy to difficult, and was given with a time limit such that only the most intelligent would answer all of them. As already mentioned, Spearman's statistical approach provided the theoretical foundation for combining such sets into a *battery* of sub-tests for measuring *g*. When America entered World War I in 1917, a group of leading psychologists including Otis, Terman, Thorndike and Yerkes was able to convince the U.S. Army of the likely value of such a group test for measuring the general ability level of recruits. Several hundred men could be tested in the time previously needed to give one Stanford-Binet test; and some $1\frac{3}{4}$ million in all took the Army Alpha or Army Beta tests during the next two years. Army Alpha consisted of eight sub-tests, each timed separately. The following are examples of the types of item[1]:

Ex. 7. *Analogies.* Leg is to knee as arm is to:
  (wrist, hand, elbow, shoulder)

  8. *Number Series.* 2 3 5 8 12 17 — —
  (Write the next two numbers in the series)

  9. *Mixed Sentences.* River London is Thames the on.
                        TRUE   FALSE

  10. *Vocabulary.* moist dry   SAME   OPPOSITE
  11.   order command SAME   OPPOSITE

Army Beta was based on non-verbal or pictorial problems, and was used for recruits unfamiliar with the English language, such as immigrants.

Note that the scoring of group tests is objective—a matter of totalling the correct responses, whereas in a Binet test the child gives his answers in his own words and the tester assesses their adequacy. Army Alpha scores were not usually translated into Mental Ages or I.Q.s, but graded arbitrarily on a letter scale from A to E (cf. Yoakum and Yerkes, 1920).

Many interesting findings arose from this vast-scale experiment, for example the differences in average scores between recruits of different national and racial descent (cf. p. 174). But

[1] Answers to these and later Examples are listed on p. 192.

doubt was soon cast on the assumption that these differences represented differences in innate intelligence, when it was noted that the highest scoring groups were also those with greatest socio-economic advancement and educational facilities. Indeed, negroes from some of the northern states of America did better than whites from some of the southern states. It was also shown that the average Army Alpha score for the total body of recruits was equivalent to a Mental Age of only 13 years. This was taken to imply that, while educational attainments and vocational knowledge or skills go on increasing till a late age, intelligence reaches its maximum during adolescence. Nowadays, however, we would ascribe this result partly to the fact that the Army tests were highly speeded (and ability to work at speed declines rapidly with age), and partly to the low level of education of a large proportion of adults in 1917, which markedly affected performance on such a verbal test. When a corresponding assessment was made in World War II, the recruits' average had risen by an amount equivalent to over 10 points of I.Q., reflecting both the improved level of education in the 1940s and the greater familiarity with tests (cf. Tuddenham, 1948).

Finally, it was found repeatedly that Army Alpha scores correlated well—to about 0·5—with assessments of the men's later proficiency at a variety of Army jobs. A higher figure would hardly be expected in view of the important part played by specialised abilities and personality qualities in vocational success.

The American Army experiment naturally gave a considerable boost to group testing, and similar tests at a level more suitable for school children, or for adults of superior ability such as college students, multiplied rapidly from 1920 onwards. In this country, Ballard published several tests and did much to gain the interest of teachers and the public by his books, *Mental Tests* (1920) and *Group Tests of Intelligence* (1922). Further impetus to the use of tests in schools was given by a Board of Education Report, *Psychological Tests of Educable Capacity* (1924). Some of Burt's tests were first introduced into the Special Place examinations for grammar school entrance in Bradford in 1919. Two years later, G. H. Thomson devised the Northumberland Mental Test and demonstrated its usefulness in picking out bright children in rural areas, whose performance in ordinary selection examinations was handicapped by poverty of background, ill-health or inefficient schooling. He also surveyed the results of over 13,000 children, classifying them by parental occupation (Duff and Thomson, 1923). Gradually more and more education authorities followed suit, and by the 1930s Moray House, Edinburgh, was producing a new intelligence test every year for their use. Increasing dissatisfaction with subjectively marked English and arithmetic papers in the scholarship examination also led many authorities to prefer Moray House, or other similar educational attainment tests.

FURTHER DEVELOPMENTS IN TESTING IN BRITAIN

American Army recruits who obtained very low scores on the group tests were often given a version of the Binet-Simon individual scale. But as this was based largely on verbal questions and answers, a series of practical performance tests, based chiefly on formboards and picture puzzles, was assembled by Pintner and Paterson in 1917 for use with men having language handicaps. This Pintner-Paterson scale was adapted by Gaw (1925) in Britain; but another collection, standardised and published by Drever and Collins in 1928, has commonly been used, e.g. with deaf children or others suspected of serious verbal deficiencies.

Soon after the 1914-1918 war, the National Institute of Industrial Psychology was founded. Here a procedure for giving guidance to adolescents or young adults on suitable careers, based on a thorough study of each individual's aptitudes and inclinations by intelligence and other tests and interview, was worked out by Burt and his collaborators. The child guidance movement, initiated by Burt's work with delinquent children in London and by Drever's and Boyd's clinics in Scotland, also expanded in the 1920s and 1930s. The Stanford-Binet, Burt's educational tests, and various performance tests were found invaluable in the detailed diagnosis of emotionally disturbed or of backward children.

The scope and application of available tests extended rapidly in America, more slowly in Britain. Scales were constructed for assessing the developmental level of pre-school children, and pictorial group tests were devised for school children from 5 up who could not read the instructions and items of the ordinary verbal test. In 1938 Penrose and Raven issued their Progressive Matrices (p. 84), which tests reasoning by means of abstract diagrammatic problems from the level of defective adults or 8-year children up to superior adult. This was adopted as the basic intelligence test by the Army and Navy personnel selection departments in 1941, and applied to several million recruits before the end of the war. The greater reliability of tests aiming to cover only a limited range of intelligence was realised by Richardson with his Simplex and Simplex Junior tests, and by R. B. Cattell with his Intelligence Scales 0, I, II, and III (the last of these being difficult enough to extend the university graduate).

In 1937, the Stanford-Binet was replaced by the new Stanford revision of Terman-Merrill test, which provided two parallel scales for individual testing from 2·0 years to superior adult levels. Though generally employed for child guidance work, the Terman-Merrill showed certain weaknesses, which are described later; and at the time of writing many clinical psychologists are adopting other scales devised in America by D. Wechsler. The Wechsler-Bellevue Scales Forms I and II and the Wechsler Adult Scale are more appropriate for adult testing, and the Wechsler Intelligence Scale for Children covers the 5–15-year range. All of these yield separate verbal and performance test I.Q.s (cf. p. 56). The late 1930s also saw the publication of Schonell's useful series of reading, spelling, arithmetic and other educational tests (Schonell, 1950). Several of these are termed 'diagnostic tests', since they are de-signed less to provide overall measures of attainment than to reveal the particular nature of a reading or arithmetical disability.

In the early days of the Second World War, little use was made of psychological tests. But by 1941 all three Services had estab-lished personnel selection departments, which constructed and applied tests of intelligence, attainments and mechanical and other aptitudes, and assisted in the allocation of recruits, in officer selection and other functions, on a scale quite unprecedented out-side America.[1] The success of these methods was amply attested by reductions in the numbers of recruits unsuitably placed, and by the fact that the departments have been retained in peace-time to undertake the assessment of regular as well as of National Service recruits. At the close of the war also, the Civil Service brought in psychological testing as part of its selection procedure for clerical officers, postal and other workers, and even for high-

[1] It should be noted, however, that tests were regarded as aids rather than as sole criteria of suitability. Each recruit also filled in a biographical questionnaire, and was interviewed, in order to bring together all the relevant information (cf. Vernon and Parry, 1949).

grade administrators. With the 1944 Education Act it was hoped to introduce allocation of all 11-year-old children to appropriate types of secondary education, rather than selection merely of the 'cream' for grammar schools. Different local education authorities vary considerably in the organisation of their secondary schools and in their allocation and selection procedures, but there are few which do not employ standardised tests at some stage.[1] Indeed, so much research time and effort has been devoted by British educational psychologists to improving and validating '11-plus' tests, and investigating other controversial aspects of selection, that progress has been slow in other important branches of testing.

Nevertheless the university Education and Psychology Departments, the National Institute of Industrial Psychology and other investigators have contributed much, by means of tests, to our knowledge of child development, of the causal factors in backwardness and in educational or vocational success, of the effects of different teaching methods, of the reliability and other statistical aspects of school marks and examinations, and of the diversity and inter-relations of human abilities. Particularly worthy of mention is the Scottish Council for Research in Education which, since 1930, has published over forty volumes of such enquiries, including the famous surveys of the intelligence of the complete 11-year-old Scottish population in 1932 and 1947. The National Foundation for Educational Research in England and Wales was founded in 1945, and its main interests include the production of tests to serve the needs of the education system, and studies of secondary school selection and of factors that promote educational progress. The Australian Council for Educational Research likewise has a highly efficient test-construction section, and several of its publications might well be of use in our own schools.

DEVELOPMENTS IN TESTING IN THE U.S.A.

All kinds of testing are so much more highly developed in America than here that we can draw attention only to one or two of the major trends (cf. Anastasi, 1954). First it is necessary to trace further the influence of Spearman's work on factor analysis.

[1] Cf. the survey of practices in 1956 by Yates and Pidgeon (1957). For a general discussion of the problems and techniques of selection, see Vernon (1957).

According to his view, g was almost the only important factor underlying people's abilities, and thus the only one worth measuring. This rather narrow conception was criticised by Thomson and Burt in Britain, and by Kelley, Thurstone and others in America. Burt, for example, showed that additional sub-types of ability could be distinguished, such as verbal or linguistic, numerical, practical, etc. Thus, given two children with the same g or general intelligence, one might be better than the other at all tasks of a strongly verbal nature, suggesting that he is superior in a v factor. Such abilities (which Spearman himself began to admit in the later 1920s and 1930s) are called *group factors*, since they run through groups of specialised tests. Thurstone went even further and, on the basis of his investigations during 1937–42, largely discarded the notion of a general intelligence, breaking it down into a series of faculties or common factors, of which the chief were V (verbal), I (inductive reasoning), D (deductive), N (numerical), S (spatial), W (word fluency), M (rote memory) and P (perceptual speed).[1] Rather than test a child's or adult's global or all-round intelligence—something which in any case could not be satisfactorily defined—he proposed to obtain a profile or graph of scores on these factors, as giving much fuller information for purposes of educational or vocational guidance. However he admitted that, among children at least, the factors themselves overlapped, i.e. that there might be some common component or components akin to Spearman's g.

Thus although American psychologists have continued to publish and use general intelligence tests, there has been a noticeable tendency to rely on more specialised tests. At college entrance, for example, most universities employ a test battery with verbal and mathematical sections (sometimes also spatial, for help in selecting engineers). And in addition to Thurstone's own Primary Mental Abilities (PMA) tests of his various factors, there are numerous series of factor tests and differential aptitude tests, aiming to measure Reasoning, Verbal, Numerical, Spatial, Clerical and other abilities. One such battery, for adolescents and adults, has been published in this country by Morrisby (1955). While we would agree that these could be very useful in theory, if the factors or aptitudes were clearly distinguishable, in practice they are far

[1] British workers have generally named their factors with small letters, g, v, n, m (mechanical), k (spatial), etc.

from satisfactory, partly because the tests do not measure the separate abilities with sufficient reliability, partly because they overlap so strongly, thus confirming Spearman's view that g (or $g + v$) is predominant in almost all abilities. When such tests are applied to secondary school pupils or college students who are taking a variety of courses, it is always the Verbal and Reasoning tests that give the highest correlations with scholastic grades; only to a slight extent do numerical, spatial or mechanical tests help to improve the predictions of mathematical, scientific, technical or other achievement.

The problem of differentiating abilities along different lines by means of objective tests is, therefore, still a very difficult one. During World War II, the American Army relied largely on a General Classification Test, which was a composite of verbal, numerical and spatial items. Numerous additional mechanical, mathematical and other tests were employed to help in allocating to special jobs in the Services, and the U.S. Air Force, in particular, developed an extensive series of printed tests and practical or psychomotor tests (e.g. of hand and eye co-ordination) for select-ing air-crew. In the post-war years, however, the Services have tried to divide up jobs into a limited number of 'aptitude areas'. For example, the Army distinguishes:

Combat jobs	Radio
Electrical and Electronic	Clerical, and
Armaments Maintenance	General Technical jobs (Military
Vehicle Maintenance	Police, Cook, etc.)

Every recruit takes a battery of 12 varied group tests, two of these having been shown to be particularly relevant to each area and less highly correlated with success in other areas. As far as possible, then, he is assigned to the area in which he scores most highly. Note that this is an *ad hoc* classification; neither the areas nor the tests represent well-defined ability factors. Differentiation also is very incomplete: many men score high, and others low, on the tests for all areas. Nevertheless it is a relatively effective system which can be applied on a large scale, and which does represent some advance over ordinary intelligence testing.

Despite the partial confirmation of Spearman's views by later research, we realise now that he was quite wrong in claiming that the conventional individual or group intelligence test supplies an almost pure measure of g, plus small s or specific components. Possibly half its content may be attributable to g, though in the case of verbal tests the v-component may be of much the same magnitude as its g. Some of the items in an individual test may further involve spatial, numerical, rote memory and other abilities; and the group test often brings in other group factors of a more formal kind, such as ability to do well at choice-response items and capacity for working at speed. Lastly, there are always the specific components and the chance elements arising from its imperfect reliability (cf. p. 111). By means of factor-analytic studies it is possible to determine roughly the relative contributions of such components, though advances in our knowledge are slow because any such study involves giving large numbers of tests to large numbers of children or adults, and even then the results vary greatly with the type of people tested and the theories held by the particular tester. Americans, for example, still do not usually admit a g factor, though their V and I or R (reasoning) factors cover much the same ground. As one moves up the scale to the superior adult level, the situation becomes still more confused. Being highly selected, college graduates show a much less pronounced range of *general* ability, and their specialised abilities at different types of test stand out more. Thus J. P. Guilford (1956), in California, has conducted a series of large-scale researches and claims to have broken down intellectual capacity into over forty factors, each defined in terms of specified tests. These include:

Eduction of several kinds of relations   Adaptive Flexibility
Foresight factors   Six types of Memory
Four kinds of Fluency   Verbal Comprehension
Evaluative and Judgment abilities   Numerical Facility
Sensitivity to Problems   Spatial Orientation
Originality   Visualisation, etc.

So far, however, there is very little evidence that tests of these alleged components of high-grade intelligence do link up with abilities for different college courses or careers any better than do general scholastic aptitude tests.

Turning to educational testing: the new-type test for measuring knowledge of school or college subjects may be said to have reached its highpoint in the Pennsylvania surveys, around 1930, by Learned and Wood (1938). The attainments of many thousands of students in different colleges were measured in their second and again in their fourth years, and the extraordinary variations, not only between different students but also between whole colleges, were revealed. For example, one-quarter of the younger groups scored higher than the average student who had had two further years of schooling. Particularly noteworthy, also in the 1930s, were the numerous standardised tests of attainment in almost every subject issued by the Co-operative Test Service for use at high school and college levels. But criticism of this type of test was rising, on the grounds that it encouraged the cramming of unrelated facts. R. W. Tyler, E. F. Lindquist and others realised the importance of the effects of testing or examining on the curriculum and teaching, and did much to show that objective test items could be devised which, instead of concentrating on factual details, required students to think, organise and apply their knowledge (Lindquist, 1951).

As early as 1921, Thorndike had included reading comprehension items in his Intelligence Test for College Entrants. Candidates were given a series of paragraphs to read, and each was followed by several new-type questions designed to show whether they could extract information from the material, and make inferences and judgments on the basis of their understanding. Such reading tests often proved to be more predictive of success in college courses than either the conventional group intelligence test or the attainment test covering knowledge of a particular subject. To an increasing extent, therefore, during the 1940s and 1950s, American educational tests have adopted complex comprehension items. In science, for example, some problem is described, certain experimental evidence given, and then multiple-choice questions require the candidate to infer solutions in the light of this evidence and of his scientific training, to indicate what further experiments are needed, and so forth. Similarly in social studies, a political speech or a cartoon may be presented and the candidate has to exercise critical judgment in drawing conclusions from the material. It is claimed that, if schools try to coach pupils to perform well at such tests, they will be teaching them effectively rather than cramming them with detailed facts. Moreover, such tests are likely to be more fair to schools whose courses in science or social studies are more adventurous, and they are less closely linked to any particular syllabus or textbook. The

Educational Testing Service at Princeton, and Lindquist at Iowa, have contributed principally to this production of tests which are educationally sound as well as statistically reliable and valid. The former organisation (which has absorbed the Co-operative Testing Service) is responsible for much of the selection of students for independent colleges, universities and graduate schools. At present it tests over a million students a year.

It is still open to doubt whether tests of this kind really bring out the students' judgment, organisation, understanding, etc., as effectively as can the essay examination, despite the great advantage of their objectivity of marking. Instead they appear to depend largely on general intelligence and vocabulary (or $V + R$ factors), and on the students' facility in coping with these complex multiple-choice items (cf. Vernon, 1958). But such questions are being actively investigated; and the care which is given in America to the development of scientific forms of examination contrasts markedly with the conservative reliance in Britain on essay examinations whose weaknesses are notorious.

One other interesting trend is the development of mechanical aids. Most large testing organisations, including many university departments which have to examine big groups of students, employ machine scoring. Instead of the pupil, student or other 'testee' ticking or underlining the right answers to multiple-choice items, he blackens an appropriate space on a special answer sheet. The sheet is fed into a machine which summates electrical currents running through the correct black marks, and so yields the total score instantaneously. An even more accurate and versatile scoring machine, operated photo-electrically, has been built by Lindquist at a cost of nearly one million dollars. High-speed electronic computing machines are also generally available to research workers, so that factorial studies of, say, 100 tests can be carried out in far less time than British psychologists would take to analyse 10 tests by hand. This may be one reason for the American's interest in a much wider variety of factors, and the British emphasis on g and a few other major types of ability.

Many other applications of testing might be mentioned, such as the selection of industrial workers and the clinical study of mental hospital patients. But enough has been said to justify the claim with which we began, that intelligence and educational testing have come to stay.

Chapter Two

THE NATURE OF INTELLIGENCE

THE word 'intelligence' goes back to Aristotle who, as Burt (1955) points out, distinguished *orexis*—the emotional and moral functions, from *dianoia*—the cognitive and intellectual functions. The latter word was translated by Cicero as *intellegentia* (*inter* within, *legere* to bring together, choose, discriminate). During the past century, however, there has been a great deal of controversy over its more precise definition, and in particular over the following points. First, is intelligence a unitary faculty of the mind? Are our diverse cognitive capacities—perceiving, thinking, imagining, learning, recalling, together with special abilities along different lines—all functions of this intelligence, or are they relatively or completely independent? Secondly, is intelligence inborn or innate, inherited from our ancestors, and therefore constant throughout life (apart from its natural growth during childhood and eventual decline with senescence); or is it partly or even wholly dependent on upbringing and education? We still lack any definition of intelligence which is acceptable to the majority of psychologists, and which might provide a sound basis for constructing intelligence tests. Nevertheless, as will appear below, the answers to both these questions have been illumined by scientific investigations with intelligence tests; and in the post-war years there seems to have been some *rapprochement* between previously conflicting approaches and the emergence of a broader and more satisfactory theory.

In 1921 a symposium was published in the American *Journal of Educational Psychology* on "Intelligence and its Measurement", in which thirteen prominent psychologists put forward thirteen largely different views. However, these, and the many other attempts to define intelligence, can be usefully grouped under three main categories, which we may call (*a*) the biological, (*b*) the psychological, (*c*) the operational.

BIOLOGICAL APPROACHES

Nearly one hundred years ago Charles Darwin and Herbert Spencer pointed out that, in the course of evolution, the increasing size and complexity of the higher brain centres had been accompanied by increasing flexibility and complexity of behaviour. In lower species we observe relatively mechanical responses to environmental stimuli, based on fixed tropisms, reflexes or complex instincts, whereas higher species, culminating in man, are more adaptable and versatile. Thus intelligence has often been defined as capacity for profiting by experience, adaptation to environment, plasticity, or ability to learn. Spencer and his followers—Lloyd Morgan, McDougall and Binet—thought of intelligence as an inherited and a general capacity. Both in the evolution of species and in the development of the individual, the various more specialised sensory, thinking and other capacities progressively differentiate or grow out of this general adaptability.

There are, however, numerous difficulties in accepting this biological conception in its original form, and further difficulties in applying it to human intelligence in practice. It is obvious, for example, that our current intelligence tests make no attempt to measure modifiability or learning capacity as such. Again, it seems curious that many people whom we would regard as highly intelligent, and who do quite well on our tests, are in fact not very well adapted to the physical and social environment in which they live (absent-minded professors, for example).

The recent work of comparative psychologists has led to considerable changes in our views on animal instinct. While re-emphasising the importance of innate mechanisms, they have shown that many features of behaviour which appear mechanical and universal to the species actually develop only under appropriate environmental stimulation; that is, they involve conditioning or learning. Again we can no longer accept a straightforward connection between complexity of adaptation and mere size or complexity of the brain. Thus spiders solve complex problems of spatial relations in making their webs, and ants learn mazes almost as readily as rats do, though far inferior in brain development. Different species, in other words, have evolved all sorts of different types of adaptation. Within the human species itself there is no connection whatever between intelligence and the size of the brain, or number of neurones, or any other physiological characteristic that has been studied so far. Only in pathological cases such as idiots, seniles and some psychotics does the brain show noticeable abnormalities. There is also the very puzzling fact that brain damage, or operations like leucotomy, and even removal of whole sections of the brain, often have no permanent effect on people's daily life adaptation or their performance at intelligence tests.

Nevertheless a generalisation along the following lines would seem acceptable in the light of modern biological and psychological knowledge: in lower species, the animal's behaviour is more directly and immediately determined either by its organic structure (innate neural and biochemical mechanisms), or by external stimulation to which it becomes conditioned, or both; whereas at higher levels, intervening processes occur to a greater extent in the central nervous system between the stimulus and the response, and these culminate in what we call thinking. Thus Köhler, in his famous work on apes, did not consider behaviour "as being intelligent when human beings or animals attain their objective by a direct, unquestionable route, which . . . arises naturally out of their organisation". 'Insight', for him, involved mental reinterpretation or restructuring of the problem situation. Such a view links up not only with the work of Hebb and Piaget, which we shall outline below, but also with practical intelligence testing. For the more complex intellectual problems which intelligent humans (or rats or apes) can solve are those that involve most internal thinking, and which make most use of abstract concepts.

PSYCHOLOGICAL DEFINITIONS

Many psychologists have been less concerned with the evolution of intelligence in the animal world than with the particular cognitive functions which are most characteristic of human intelligence. Arguments have been advanced for a great variety of mental faculties, including planning ability, foresight, originality and problem solving. Terman particularly emphasised capacity for abstract thinking. Binet frankly regarded intelligence as a complex set of qualities, including:

(i) the appreciation of a problem and the direction of the mind towards its execution; (ii) the capacity for making the necessary adaptations to reach a definite end; (iii) the power of self-criticism.

Elsewhere he writes that the fundamental quality is "judgment, otherwise called good sense, practical sense, initiative, the faculty of adapting oneself to circumstances. To judge well, to comprehend well, to reason well, these are the essential activities of intelligence."

Spearman, as we have seen, interpreted g as "the eduction of relations and correlates", and Knight (1943) expands this into his definition of intelligence as "the capacity of relational, constructive thinking, directed to the attainment of some end". Like most writers, he distinguishes this from acquired knowledge or skills. The acquisition of these often involves grasping new relationships; hence most educational tests correlate highly with intelligence tests. But they also depend on how much the individual has been taught, and on his retentivity, which are clearly different from his intelligence. Knight also criticises Binet's inclusion of such qualities as 'self-criticism' and 'initiative', since these belong more to temperament or character than to intellect. And he objects to Thorndike's attempt to reduce intelligence to the number of associations, or brain connections, which underlie ideas; for one can use associations in such unintelligent mental activities as reproductive or mechanical thinking, or in uncontrolled fantasy and day-dreaming.

Perhaps the most striking feature of these different views is not that they disagree but that all the functions listed overlap considerably, and may indeed be regarded as partial aspects of intelligence. At the same time no definition is precise enough to provide much guidance in devising intelligence tests. A test item which seemed to one psychologist to involve abstract thinking might or might not be regarded by another as measuring judgment or grasping relationships, and so on.

OPERATIONAL APPROACHES[1]

Since theoretical discussions about the nature of intelligence do not seem to get us anywhere, other writers have tried to dismiss the problem by claiming that "intelligence is what intelligence tests measure". They point out that we can measure electricity without being able to define its precise nature. And just as

[1] Operational means—definable in terms of concrete operations, such as scores on mental tests; it corresponds, in other words, to Behaviouristic, and it avoids the assumption of mental entities which cannot be directly observed or measured.

electricity can be put to practical uses because we can control and measure it, so we can construct and apply intelligence tests provided we can demonstrate that they enable us to make certain predictions about children and adults. It is questionable, however, whether we would ever have reached the stage of making useful predictions had not Binet and his successors had some psychological theories regarding what they were trying to measure.

Spearman, too, as we have seen, believed that g was operationally definable—a factor which emerged from analysing the correlations between tests, regardless of the particular abilities tested or the theories on which they were based. And whether or not one accepts his notion of g, one cannot gainsay the fact of positive overlapping between all abilities. Any satisfactory theory of intelligence must be able to explain why it is that the child or adult who is superior in reasoning problems is also likely to be above average, not only in memorising and vocabulary but also in arithmetic, mechanical comprehension, and even in handwriting, reaction time and sensory discrimination.[1] Another finding from Spearman's work which is fully substantiated is the existence of a kind of hierarchy of abilities, in the sense that the more complex intellectual functions generally show stronger overlapping—or a greater involvement of his g-factor—than do the simpler, rote, cognitive functions and sensory-motor capacities.

Beyond this, however, he did not succeed in determining the nature of intelligence by statistical analysis. His approach broke down, both because the general factor obtained from any battery of tests is biased by the kinds of tests used (cf. p. 181), and because it is entirely legitimate to emphasise—as Thurstone and Guilford do—the diversity as well as the generality of abilities. Different types of mental functions and different specialised aptitudes are at least partially distinguishable, despite their positive overlapping. Thus it is more consistent with the statistical evidence to think of intelligence as a fluid collection of abilities, comprising the whole of mental life, though most prominently manifest in higher relational thinking. It is a kind of average which cannot be pinned down to any single mental faculty either by psychological or statistical analysis; and inevitably it is liable to differ somewhat

[1] Admittedly correlations among the latter tests may sometimes sink to zero or even negative values, but usually only in small and highly selected groups.

according to what different psychologists choose to include within it. Probably, therefore, the best definition we can give is a rather simple, non-specific one, such as 'all-round thinking capacities', or 'mental efficiency' or, as Burt and Ballard suggest, 'general mental ability'.

THE DEVELOPMENTAL APPROACH

In recent years our conceptions of intelligence and its development have been revolutionised through the work of D. O. Hebb (1948) and J. Piaget (1950).[1] Though their approaches are very different—Hebb being interested primarily in animal psychology and brain physiology, Piaget rather in child psychology and formal logic—yet their conclusions are remarkably concordant. Their writings are also highly technical, and the following simplified exposition cannot possibly do them justice.

Both are concerned to show how the infant, whose primitive consciousness is probably completely undifferentiated, comes to perceive a world of objects independent of himself. The modes of perceiving and thinking which we as adults carry out so automatically that they seem to us part of the natural order of things, are really complex acquisitions of early childhood, each having a long history. For example, Hebb casts doubt on the Gestalt psychologists' claim that the human infant immediately perceives a square shape as a unified structure or whole. By his second year he may do so, but this is because he has had a vast number of visual experiences of square shapes seen at different distances and angles; these have been combined with muscular explorations which give the shape its consistent structure. He has to learn, again, that objects usually stay in the same position and retain the same size when he stops looking at them; that an impression of a large object partially blocking out a smaller one probably means that the former is nearer, and so on. Piaget describes the stages through which the child passes as he gradually disentangles the world by continuous experimentation, and builds up the sensory-motor schemata or patterns of response to external stimuli. Hebb argues that these experiences in the first year or so of life lead to the formation of groupings or 'assemblies' of neurones in the associa-

[1] Piaget's main contributions consist of about a dozen books, published since the war and some of them not yet translated, not the earlier and better-known works of the 1920s. A useful exposition is given by Berlyne (1957).

tion areas of the brain. The fully developed perception or idea involves an autonomous activity or cerebral discharge within the neurones, which he calls a 'phase sequence'. Note that this is by no means the same theory as the old associationist view of lowered synaptic resistances or engrams which thought of the brain as an inert transmitting system that was merely activated by incoming sensory stimuli. Nevertheless, Hebb's neurological explanations are somewhat speculative, and the present writer would prefer to substitute the psychological term 'schema' for 'phase-sequence' and to regard it as the fundamental unit of perceiving and thinking.

The schema, as described by F. C. Bartlett and apparently taken over by Piaget, is a kind of mental pattern or framework in which all our past experience relevant to the percept or concept is integrated, so that as each new impression enters consciousness, it is charged with all that has gone before. Thus, for example, a square box comes to be recognised as such more or less regardless of the distance, the angle of viewing or the surrounding background. And the world acquires those characteristics of stability, constancy and structure to which Gestalt psychologists have drawn attention.

An important feature of Hebb's views is that most perceptual schemata must be acquired at a suitable time if further mental development is to be possible. Experiments on apes brought up in the dark, and studies of persons born blind and given sight by later operations for cataract, show what extreme difficulties they have in building up for themselves intelligible visual perceptions of the world. (However, the validity of this evidence has been disputed.) Schemata depend, too, on wide and varied visual and kinaesthetic sensations. The animal or human infant needs to explore the environment and gain familiarity with sizes and shapes, and spatial and temporal relations, to find out how the world 'works'; and to do this he requires an atmosphere of security and freedom. Rats or dogs brought up as pets with the free run of a rich environment are found to be more intelligent—better at learning and problem-solving—when they reach maturity than those reared in the more restricted environment of a cage. The implications of this for the development of human intelligence are obvious. These early schemata are the bases for the far more elaborate learning of which man is capable than other animals.

Thus it is highly probable that poverty of early perceptual experience, or feelings of emotional insecurity, may sensibly affect the child's whole intellectual growth. Such factors may, for instance, underlie to some extent the differences in intelligence between the middle-class and the slum child.

The early perceptual schemata become organised into 'higher-order' ones—concepts or ideas—which to a still greater extent operate as autonomous units in the association areas of the brain. Once they are established they become independent of particular neurones or brain pathways, according to Hebb, and are therefore largely unaffected by serious brain injuries or operations. Thus mental efficiency in everyday affairs, and correct responses to Binet test items, frequently survive extensive brain damage. But the capacity for building up entirely new schemata (which can be partially tested by so-called 'concept formation' tests) does show greater signs of deterioration.

One other valuable point made by Hebb is his distinction between Intelligence A—genetic potentiality—and Intelligence B, present mental efficiency. The former represents the capacity of the central nervous system for forming, retaining and recombining schemata, and it is ultimately determined by the genes: whereas the latter represents the cognitive abilities which have been built up during infancy and childhood, and which do not develop in the absence of suitable environmental stimulation. Intelligence A is hypothetical only; we cannot directly observe or measure it. Nevertheless, as shown in Chapter Nine, there is strong evidence for its existence. Indeed some psychologists, such as Burt and R. B. Cattell, wish to retain the term intelligence for the basic inborn capacity. We would prefer, however, to apply it to the ability which can be observed in daily life, at school or at work, and which is sampled fairly effectively by our tests; and this is the product of heredity and upbringing. Although, as we shall see later, there is still considerable controversy regarding the relative influence of nature and nurture, the great majority of psychologists would nowadays agree that the intelligence we measure should not be interpreted as pure inborn ability.

LANGUAGE AND THE SOCIALISATION OF THINKING

Piaget describes how imagery and thinking grow out of overt trial-and-error behaviour. Even a child of 2, say, wishing to reach a toy from a high shelf, begins to abbreviate his actions. Instead of reaching, and then getting a chair to raise himself on, he carries out the earlier stages mentally and goes straight for a large enough chair; in other words, he has acquired a schema which fits this type of problem situation. During the second and later years also, language comes to play an increasing part. First it helps in the classification and stabilisation of his perceptions. Objects or events become identified and sorted out when they are given distinct names. Secondly, words provide labels or symbols for concepts, that is, for clusters of things or actions. Thus if his mother says: "Hot, don't touch", he can at once react appropriately on the basis of schemata that may have been acquired in some quite different context. Thirdly, language is used by society to pass on its conceptions of the world to the next generation. 'Sport', for example, describes not merely certain activities and institutions, but also an attitude of mind which is quite different in England from what it would be in France or Russia or Polynesia. And fourthly, language has been defined as a set of rules for saying things that have *not* been said before, as when a boy recombines previously acquired linguistic schemata to write a school composition or to plan an exploit with his gang. Thought and the exercise of intelligence can, of course, occur without the use of words, but it is clear that intelligent thinking can develop only in a social context, where adults and older children, either at home or at school, help to enrich the child's stock of percepts and concepts and to clarify the relations between them through speech. Moreover, the highest achievements of intellect in the creative writer or scientist generally seem to be carried out in terms of verbal, numerical or similar symbols. Thus intelligence could hardly develop without this tool that the growing child acquires from the society in which he is reared.

At the same time, Piaget insists that intelligence is no one distinctive faculty—it cannot be reduced to, say, grasping of relations or abstract thinking; it is present in all adaptations of lower animals as well as of infants and mature adults. Behaviour becomes progressively more intelligent the more complex the 'lines of interaction' between organism and environment, or as Hebb would say—the greater the amount of autonomous cerebral activity. In the child's early years his behaviour consists predominantly of concrete and direct reactions to practical experience, and these sensory-motor adaptations tend to be one-way and inflexible, i.e. unintelligent. At the higher stages, culminating in abstract, logical reasoning, the individual's thinking is characterised by mobility—the capacity to transfer to new situations, flexibility and reversibility—or ease of manipulation of ideas.

In between the sensory-motor and the logical stages comes an egocentric stage, when the child's conceptions of space, time, causation, morality, etc., are largely irrational, inconsistent and intuitive, bound up with his own needs and interests. Even in the company of other children or adults he hardly realises, at 5 years or so, that other people's views of the world can differ from his own; whereas by 15, even when thinking in solitude, his conceptions are socially determined and follow a rational pattern which he expects to be acceptable to others. The egocentric stage is characterised by animism and magical interpretations, syncretism (things that happen to occur together are mutually explanatory) rather than mechanistic causality, arguing by analogy, and tolerance of contradictions.

We should point out, however, that many psychologists disagree with Piaget's notion of children passing through definite stages of concept development at particular ages. True, he lays more stress on the regular succession than on the actual month or year in which the stage appears. But he seems too apt to attribute such development to internal maturation—that is, to hereditary factors—although at other times he admits the importance of contacts with the real world and people in fashioning logical thinking. Further, he neglects the tremendous variations in level of development among different children at the same age. Indeed, subsequent investigations have shown, as we might have expected, that the stages are more closely associated with Mental Age than with Chronological Age. But over and above this there are great variations among different kinds of ideas and different thinking situations; that is, egocentrism is not so much a natural stage of childhood as a stage in the development of each class of ideas. It persists among the majority of adults (even those of superior education and intelligence) when they are thinking about economic, political, social and religious matters, or bringing up of children, or about personal relations with other people. Much the same illogicalities and prejudices that Piaget attributed to childhood are described, among adults, in Thouless's book *Straight and*

Crooked Thinking (1930). The average adult's concepts and thinking attain a fair degree of rationality when emotions are not involved, or when the exigences of the physical world have forced him to be objective—as, for example, in dealing with temporal and spatial problems involved in getting to his job on time. But equally, children much younger than 5 seem to reach the rational stage in some of their practical activities, say in block-building or in manipulating furniture to reach a desired object.

This point is an important one since the traditional distinction between cognitive and affective aspects of mental life has often been carried too far. Intellectual conceptions and reasoning do not develop in isolation, as it were. Yet in trying to measure intelligence we are artificially abstracting intellectual competence from the context of sentiments and complexes in which it normally manifests itself. However, there is some justification for this in that our thinking about non-controversial matters usually is logical, and intelligence tests can be devised within this area and thus avoid egocentric thinking. We shall see later that, among normal children and adults, their results seem to be remarkably little affected by motivation or emotion. Even the neurotic adult does not, on average, score lower than normal, though at the same time intelligence does generally correlate positively with superior character traits. There is some evidence, also, that work-attitude factors such as persistence and carefulness have a more marked effect on test performance when the test items are either very difficult or very easy (cf. p. 182). It is among pre-school children and psychotic adults that the influence of emotional dispositions on intellectual functioning is most obvious; and in such cases it is essential that any testing be conducted by a skilled child psychologist or clinical psychologist who can, to some extent, allow for and control these influences.

THE PSYCHOLOGY OF THINKING

We have already stressed the importance of concepts and rules which can be transferred to a wide variety of situations. While mental development certainly includes the acquisition of information, at least as necessary is the acquisition of methods of tackling the sorts of problems people meet in daily life, or at school, or in intelligence tests. Harlow (1949) has demonstrated the same principle in monkeys: given a series of discrimination problems, their ability to solve them progressively improved. They had "learned how to learn". "This learning to learn transforms the organism from a creature that adapts to a changing environment by trial and error to one that adapts by seeming hypothesis and insight."

However this is not the whole story. In his recent book (1958), F. C. Bartlett brings out the variety and complexity of thinking processes. He shows that, while the term 'thinking' can be applied to almost any mental process which is not merely a response to external stimuli, it is characterised in particular by the 'filling in of gaps'. That is to say, the thinker takes in contributory sources of evidence and combines these with recalled information. But in order to reach a solution he has to interpolate or extrapolate from the evidence, or else reinterpret it and see it in a new light (cf. Köhler's account of 'insight'). Bartlett draws attention to the importance of transferring any rules, regularities, sequences or generalisations that have been used in previous situations, but points out that this is also one of the most frequent sources of erroneous thinking. Indeed, the less intelligent often require more contributory evidence than the brighter individual to 'jolt them out of' inappropriate techniques. Especially in everyday thinking about human affairs, we are apt to make use of conventional generalisations, stereotypes and personal experience rather than use the evidence actually available—a point which has also been well brought out by G. W. Allport in his book on *The Nature of Prejudice* (1954).

Elsewhere the present writer has suggested that the same conception applies at all stages of mental growth. Each schema that we acquire not only provides a basis for further development, but also tends in itself to become stereotyped or rigid, and thus to inhibit further development or reintegration. Thus all-round mental efficiency or Intelligence B depends not only on the total number and complexity of schemata, but also on the degree to which we are able to differentiate or break them down and keep them flexible. And it is this aspect which has repeatedly been shown to be impaired by certain types of brain injury and by ageing. The adult of, say, 50 may have a far wider stock of concepts and techniques for thinking than the 20-year old, and yet be relatively less successful in applying them to unfamiliar reasoning problems. This flexibility aspect of intelligence is also affected by personality qualities such as authoritarianism *vs.* tolerance, and is thus dependent on the success or failure of early upbringing and of schooling in encouraging initiative, originality and rationality of ideas.

Bartlett also offers a useful classification of different species of thinking. Thus he distinguishes thinking in closed systems, where the correct solution is predetermined and the individual has to use the evidence to find the right steps for filling in a limited number of gaps, from adventurous thinking, where there is freedom of method and the thinker cannot know whether his solution is the correct or final one. In the latter category he describes the differences between everyday, scientific, artistic and other kinds of thought. Intelligence test items, even of the individually administered Binet type, necessarily belong to the former category, and therefore omit such aspects of thinking as sensitivity to problems, imaginativeness, and what we call 'wisdom' or good judgment. However, it is noteworthy that all these qualities have been studied by Guilford (cf. p. 24), though it is not yet clear how far his factors are really distinctive, or representative of thinking in real-life situations.

INTELLIGENCE AND ATTAINMENTS

We have arrived at the view that intelligence corresponds to the general level of complexity and flexibility of a person's schemata, which have been built up cumulatively in the course of his lifetime. It would follow that no sharp distinction should be drawn between intelligence and attainments; nor should we think of the former as one of the main causal factors in determining the latter. Both are dependent on, or limited by, genetic factors, that is Intelligence A; and it is probable that various specialised attainments involve particular genes in addition—e.g. those underlying musical or numerical talents. But there is no essential difference between the acquisition of, say, reading skills and the acquisition of reasoning or other capacities which would be conventionally regarded as part of intelligence. Both involve the development of schemata through exercise with appropriate materials, and their shaping or correcting by environmental pressures.

We have been too apt to think of attainments as wholly learned and dependent mainly on goodness of schooling. Many investigations have shown that the amount of time given to teaching a subject in different schools has little connection with the amount acquired. True, the use of improved educational techniques can usually be shown experimentally to bring about greater gains, but the contribution they make is always a small one relative to the total range of variations in attainment. We recognise the importance of genetic factors and of general developmental level when we talk of 'reading readiness'. Similarly, in arithmetic the learning of multiplication tables does not consist merely in the accretion of bits of information through repeated drilling. Certainly practice is necessary, as it is in the development of our percepts and concepts and techniques of thinking. But for progress to occur it is equally necessary for children to explore and discover relations among numbers, in and out of school.

Nevertheless, a relative distinction still seems useful. Attainments refer to mental knowledge, skills and understandings which are more directly channelled by the content of the curriculum and the kind of training the school (or other instruction) provides, and which probably depend to a greater extent on interests and on personality qualities such as industry. On the other hand, intelligence refers to the more generalised thinking functions—all-round conceptual development, techniques of analysing, comprehending, organising, learning and problem-solving which—as Ferguson (1954) points out—have crystallised out of the child's previous experience in or out of school, and which can be transferred to a wider variety of new situations.

Many abilities are intermediate and therefore difficult to classify under either heading. Vocabulary, for example, often turns up either in intelligence or in English attainment tests; general information was included in the Army Alpha test; and problem arithmetic is known to be one of the best tests of Thurstone's inductive reasoning factor. As pointed out above (p. 25), many American educational psychologists have abandoned *both* intelligence and ordinary attainment tests at the senior high school and college levels, and prefer to try to measure what they call 'developed abilities', such as reasoning with mathematical, linguistic, scientific or social studies materials. The layman might suppose that breadth of vocabulary depends mainly on what children are taught by their parents and school teachers; and indeed, children from middle-class, and particularly from professional, homes, where they hear richer and more accurate speech, do tend to show better vocabulary than children from working-class homes. But in fact neither example nor instruction is likely to enable them to define and use difficult words correctly unless they have reached a sufficiently advanced stage of mental development to understand the underlying concepts.

CONCLUSION

We must now try to link up our developmental psychological theory with the findings of factor analysis. Although cognitive functions are almost infinitely varied, g can be regarded as the highest common factor among, or as the overall efficiency of, schemata. This view is very similar to that of G. H. Thomson (1939), one of Spearman's earliest critics. He condemned the tendency to regard statistically derived factors as unitary powers or organs of the mind, and instead thought of the mind as consisting of an immense number of bonds or associations. Any one mental test would involve the operation of many such bonds, and two or more tests would tend to correlate because they draw on the same total 'pool'. We can now see several reasons for expecting positive overlapping among all cognitive tests. First there is some innate quality of the human nervous system which makes men more capable than lower animals of acquiring, breaking up and recombining habits, percepts, concepts and schemata of all kinds; and some individuals have greater genetic potentiality than others.

Secondly, the essentially cumulative nature of mental growth implies that those who early in life acquire a larger stock of perceptual schemata and verbal habits, are better able to build up more complex and more flexible schemata necessary for conceptual thinking. Moreover, the later-developed, higher-order ones will naturally be more inclusive or more g-saturated, whereas the earlier sensory and motor ones will appear relatively differentiated and specific. Thirdly, some individuals are reared in a richer, more stimulating and more emotionally adjusting environment than others, and this contributes throughout childhood, adolescence and early adulthood to the abilities they manifest in almost any kind of test. Others are relatively starved or emotionally frustrated, so that they fail to throw off the emotional components of primitive thinking; or their schemata become set and rigid, thus inhibiting the acquisition of new ones; and their overall intellectual efficiency begins to decline, perhaps even before they have grown to full maturity.

Finally, it should be noted that g or Intelligence B should not be regarded as something constant in composition throughout the life span. Bayley's (1940) detailed studies of 0–3-year-old children show us a multiplicity of functions growing more or less independently out of previously maturing functions. Through the interplay of schemata and through the pervasive influence of language, a considerable degree of unification emerges. But children's activities, experiences and interests vary so much that different kinds of ideas and different skills often show very uneven development. We would agree, too, with Piaget's notion that the characteristic thinking processes alter greatly in quality, as well as in overall efficiency, as children get older. Such specialisation and differentiation naturally continue into adulthood; indeed, the whole conception of a 'general' intelligence becomes less applicable among adults, since their maximum capacities are expressed mainly in diverse vocational and social skills and in leisure pursuits. Hence ordinary intelligence tests, based rather on linguistic concept development and abstract reasoning, provide a less representative sampling of their schemata or, in other words, tell us less about an adult than they do about a child.

Chapter Three

ELEMENTARY PRINCIPLES OF TESTING[1]

THE view has often been expressed—by philosophers and some psychologists, as well as by laymen—that human qualities are in their very nature immeasurable. True, one cannot lay a ruler alongside a child's intelligence or perseverance or musical aptitude. Yet the notion of *more* or *less* is continually employed in human affairs. Every mother rejoices at her 3- or 4-year old's *progress* in vocabulary, and observes that he is *better* or *worse* behaved than her neighbour's children. An Army sergeant is *more* proficient or experienced than a corporal. School examinations may have their undesirable features, but *passes* and *fails*, *percentages* and other marks and degree *classes* have become part and parcel of the educational system. The psychometrist—that is the psychologist interested in mental measurement—is simply trying to turn these relatively vague quantities into purer and more precise ones. Many mental tests are, in fact, very similar to examinations, though certain precautions are taken to ensure greater accuracy. Others more closely resemble the sort of tasks or situations which we use informally when judging people's traits and abilities in everyday life. For example, a child's capacity for making a construction with bricks or blocks, or the extent of his vocabulary, have been directly adapted as part-tests of intelligence in the Terman, Wechsler and other scales. Let us, however, review the chief characteristics that distinguish the mental test from the unstandardised situations of daily life, or from school examining.

STANDARDISATION[2] OF THE TEST SITUATION AND SCORING

It is essential that the test as a whole, and its component items, together with their manner of application, should be uniform for

[1] Fuller treatment of this topic may be found in the present writer's *The Measurement of Abilities* (1956). A helpful account of the different species of measurement, some of which are, and others are not, applicable in psychology, is given by Banks and Burt (1953).

[2] The term 'standardisation' sometimes implies that test norms or standards are provided; here, however, we are using it to describe uniformity in, and control over, the conditions of application of a test and its scoring.

all 'testees' (that is, persons taking the test). Inexperienced testers sometimes think that minor alterations do not matter. For example, they may 'translate' an American test or add to the instructions in the hope of making things clearer, or not bother to adhere strictly to the time limits. But all these changes in fact make the test a new one to which the original norms (cf. p. 48) probably do not apply. All reputable tests are published with manuals giving instructions for their application which must be followed precisely.

The scoring of success or failure at each item in the test is likewise standardised or objective, in the sense that the personal judgment of the tester is kept to a minimum. This is in marked contrast to the typical school examination. As described in Chapter One, the group intelligence or educational test generally consists of multiple-choice or new-type items, so that the testee's score is simply the number of items in which the correct answer is picked from the alternatives provided. Indeed, scoring can often be done by machine.

In some scholastic tests, such as arithmetic and spelling, the child may write his own answers, since these can be scored right or wrong. Partial credits are not given, as these would introduce subjective judgment. There are a few group intelligence tests also which use creative responses.[1] Quantitative scores on practical performance tests are usually obtained by recording the number of blocks or pieces of a puzzle put together, or the number of graded problems correctly solved in a given time, or the number of seconds needed to complete a task.

However, in most individual Binet-type tests the responses are quite unrestricted, and here the manual lays down exactly what responses are acceptable or unacceptable. For example, the answer to a Stanford-Binet 8-year comprehension item: "What's the thing for you to do when you have broken something which belongs to someone else?" must imply restitution or apology; shame or confession are not sufficient by themselves.

It should hardly be necessary to point out that these or other scoring instructions should be followed implicitly. Yet, in the days before doctors were trained to apply Terman-Merrill properly, children were sometimes wrongly certified as defective through bad scoring. And it is still possible to fail 'the 11-plus' through mis-

[1] For instance: Ex. 8 (p. 17), Ex. 13 (p. 76), Ex. 43 (p. 82).

scoring a Moray House group test (e.g. missing out a couple of pages), though this is improbable since careful checking is generally applied.

At the same time, the objective conditions of giving and scoring are not everything. Both in individual and group testing, the good tester tries to ensure beforehand that each child is well motivated to do his best, avoids distracting stimuli and encourages frequently throughout.

TEST RELIABILITY AND VALIDITY

The test must be sufficiently extensive, and its component items well chosen, to yield a trustworthy or stable total score. Psychologists use the term 'reliable' if the test gives the same, or nearly the same, results when applied on two or more occasions or by two different testers; or if a closely parallel test is concordant (cf. Cronbach, 1949). No mental test is perfectly reliable in this sense, since human beings naturally vary in their responses on different occasions, or to different, though parallel, sets of items. The ordinary school essay or examination is particularly unreliable, not only because the marks are dependent on the examiner's subjective judgment, but also because pupils write better on some topics than on others.

Most published tests consist of items which have been tried out beforehand, both in order to ensure that the desired range of difficulty is covered and to see that each one gives results consistent with the results of the test as a whole. Items that fail to discriminate good from poor scorers probably contain unsuspected ambiguities, and they are either revised or eliminated. We cannot discuss here the detailed techniques of test construction, but we should note that the initial formulation of items, the trials and revisions and the eventual standardisation of a test are extremely intricate (cf. Anstey, 1948; Vernon, 1948). It is said to take some three years to produce a Moray House test. This, of course, is one reason why tests usually work better than conventional school examinations. An account of the factors that influence a test's unreliability is given in Chapter Seven.

Note that reliability does *not* mean the accuracy of the test in measuring the ability it is supposed to measure, only the dependability of the instrument itself. The accuracy or value of the test is called its validity. Thus a child's height can be measured with almost perfect reliability, but it has very little validity as a measure of his mental capacity and only a moderate validity as an index of his overall physical development. Clearly a test can have different validities for different purposes, and there are several ways of establishing these.

Inspection and analysis of the content of the test is sometimes sufficient. For example, it is obvious that a spelling test consisting of sample words of the kind that children need to use, but frequently mis-spell, has validity. Yet even here we know from experimental researches that dictation tests of sample words do not measure quite the same ability as is involved when children write compositions with few, or many, spelling errors (p. 97); also that a multiple-choice test where children have to underline the correctly spelled version among several mis-spelled versions of the same word has almost as high a validity as does a dictation-type test, although—to mere inspection—it might appear considerably less valid. Introspections from testees regarding the processes they use in answering a test also sometimes provide useful evidence.

Once we get beyond the elementary educational level, apparent or 'face' validity may be a very poor guide, particularly when adults try to judge whether or not a test measures certain qualities in children. Numerous tests of vocational aptitude which appear to involve, say, manual dexterity, carefulness, etc., have proved quite useless. Again it is dubious whether the modern complex tests (p. 25) of comprehension of paragraphs, designed to evoke judgment, logical inference, critical thinking and so forth achieve their aim (cf. Vernon, 1958). Particularly in the case of the intelligence test neither the opinion of the psychologist who devises the test, nor that of the testees, can decide whether the items are valid or not. The judgments of some critics, to the effect that Moray House tests measure 'slickness' or other such qualities, not genuine intelligence, are entirely worthless in the absence of experimental evidence.

Normally, therefore, one would prefer to have external and objective proof that a test picks out individuals with the desired qualities—for example, that a test of technical aptitude correlates with subsequent success in technical courses or jobs. Yet this approach, too, is less straightforward than might be supposed, partly because it is often difficult to get a satisfactory criterion of the qualities the test is supposed to measure. Thus no one has ever been able to validate university Arts degrees, since there is no agreement as to the ultimate objective of an Arts course and no means of ascertaining which graduates have been successful or unsuccessful subsequently in this respect. Often, too, the correlation between a test and a criterion is less important than the fact that the test adds something to already available data, or helps to differentiate the testees' suitability for two or more different outcomes. Thus a technical aptitude test which gave the same predictions as intelligence and arithmetic tests at 11-plus, or which correlated as highly with grammar school as with technical school performance, would be of little value (cf. Chapter Seven).

Here, too, intelligence tests are specially tricky because of the lack of any definitive criterion. Teachers' judgments of children have sometimes been used, but are unsatisfactory since they do not readily distinguish intelligence from scholastic success or from good classroom behaviour. Indeed, the main object of such tests is to provide a means of assessment which is independent of subjective judgment. Although Binet, in constructing his original scales, did in fact attempt to choose tasks which differentiated children called intelligent by their teachers from those called dull, he also aimed—as we have seen—at items which appeared representative of children's higher mental development, and ensured that each one was passed by greater proportions of older than of younger children. Nevertheless these criteria are insufficient; for example, they might be met by asking 'What is 7×9?', which would hardly be accepted by most people as a good test of intelligence.

The most appropriate approach in such circumstances is known as *Construct Validation*. By this is implied that the psychologist designs a test to measure a certain hypothetical quality or 'construct' and, in the absence of satisfactory external validation, seeks indirect evidence that the theory underlying his test is sound. Thus Spearman put forward the g factor as a theory to explain the correlations among varied cognitive tests, and was able to show by factor analysis that tests involving abstraction and other higher intellectual processes were highly saturated with g. The later developments that we have described have led to modifications in the theory, but factor analysis is still the chief tool employed in determining how far a test measures g, or v, or other hypothetical components. Suppose, now, that someone proposes to test a quality such as judgment, he would first make up several tests that appeared to involve this faculty, and would then have to show that these correlated among themselves, and prove that they did measure something in common over and above what could be attributable to g or V or R or other well-established factors. The results should also correlate with teachers' assessments of their students' judgment, though this evidence would not be very convincing because of the difficulties of defining and rating the quality. It might be more useful if students taught in courses specifically aimed to improve their judgment showed higher gains in test scores than those taught in more conventional courses.

It will be seen, then, that the validity of a test is a complex conception which seldom admits of a single clear answer.

TEST NORMS

Neither the number of items a child accomplishes in an intelligence or attainment test, nor other scores or examination marks, have any meaning in themselves. They must always be compared with some standard or norm derived from the performances of other similar children, e.g. with the scores of an unselected or representative age group. And so the system of expressing abilities in terms of Mental or Educational Ages and quotients was invented by Binet, Thorndike and Terman. It should be noted that norms do not attempt to set a standard of what children *should* do, but simply represent what children in general *do* do under present conditions of upbringing and schooling. Thus, for example, an average 10-year old will obtain a Word Reading Age of 10 and an English Composition Age of 10, regardless of anybody's opinion that 10-year olds can read aloud adequately but cannot write good compositions.

Although the adoption of age units provided a valuable and meaningful way of specifying abilities numerically, it has certain weaknesses, particularly among adolescents and adults. An alternative system, with quite a different basis, is that of *percentiles*. A percentile is not a percentage mark, but is the score below which falls a certain percentage of testees. Thus the 90th percentile score on any test for, say, young adults, is the score that divides (as nearly as possible) the top 10 per cent of a representative group of young adults from the bottom 90 per cent. The 50th percentile is the mark halfway down the list, often called the median. If we are told a series of percentiles for a test such as the 98th, 90th, 75th, 50th, 25th, 10th and 2nd, we can readily interpret whether any person's original or 'raw' score represents a good, average or weak performance. In effect, then, percentiles provide the same information as would I.Q.s or E.Q.s ranging from about 130, through 100 down to 70, or the same as the number of years by which a child's M.A. or E.A. exceeds or falls short of his C.A.

This system is particularly convenient when it is difficult to secure complete age groups for standardisation purposes. Indeed, it is often more useful to know the percentiles for, say, 14-year olds in secondary modern schools and the (different) percentiles for 14-year olds in typical grammar schools, than it is to have norms for 14-year olds in general.

The National Institute of Industrial Psychology issues percentile norms in different types of school for most of its group tests. Again, the British Army standardises its tests mainly in terms of percentiles for unselected recruits or for officer-candidate populations. Scores at the 90th percentile or above are referred to as S.G. (Selection Grade) I; 90th to 70th as S.G. II; 70th to 50th as III+; 50th to 30th as III−; 30th to 10th as IV; and scores obtained by the bottom 10 per cent as S.G.V. By this coarse, yet quite effective and easily intelligible, method a recruit's results on a series of diverse tests all becomes comparable. For example, a man with S.G. I or II on verbal, clerical and arithmetic tests, but S.G. IV on mechanical tests, would be better allocated to a clerical than a practical-mechanical job. Had we, however, merely known his 'raw' test scores, no such comparison would be possible. And the same is true of pupils' and students' examination marks in different subjects, since these are seldom standardised in any way; they merely reflect the particular examiners' opinions of what levels of ability should be labelled 70 per cent or 50 per cent, or 1st class or fail, etc.

When percentiles can be obtained from representative age groups, it is possible to convert them directly into equivalent I.Q.s or E.Q.s if desired, without the intervention of Mental and Educational Ages; and this is roughly the procedure adopted in the various Wechsler scales and the Moray House, National Foundation for Educational Research and other modern tests of intelligence and attainments. For example, in standardising a test at the 11-plus level, it is given to a large, representative group aged 10:0 to 12:0, subdivided into month-groups (10:0, 10:1, 10:2, etc.). Certain percentiles are extracted from each month-group, plotted on a graph and smoothed. Now it is known that approximately the top $2\frac{1}{2}$ per cent of children normally obtain I.Q.s of 130 upwards; the top 9 per cent obtain 120 upwards, and so on all down the scale. Thus the $97\frac{1}{2}$ percentile line or curve on the graph gives the 130 I.Q. (or E.Q.) norm for children of any age from 10 to 12, and the 91st percentile curve yields the 120 I.Q. norm, and so on. A conversion table is then drawn up from which may be read off the quotient corresponding to each score at each age. Actually, however, these are not quotients at all, since at no stage are M.A.s or E.A.s involved. As the authors of the tests point out, they are *standard* or *sigma scores*, to use the psychometric term.[1] Alternatively they are referred to as *deviation* I.Q.s, to distinguish them from *classical* I.Q.s. Nevertheless, in secondary school selection they are usually referred to as intelligence (or English or arithmetic) quotients and are at least as meaningful as such quotients.

If it is desired to express adult test results in terms of quotients, this is the only reasonable way of doing so. Strictly speaking, no mental test can yield a M.A. or E.A. much above 15 since, as we have seen, the average performance of persons aged over 15 years is little if any better than that of 15-year olds. The Terman-Merrill, and some other tests, are actually scored up to higher ages, and these are used to calculate quotients. But such units for expressing above-average performance are arbitrary and virtually meaningless; it would be much better to substitute deviation quotients (or percentiles).

Certain other types of test norms are occasionally used. For example, American and Australian educational tests frequently quote Grade, instead of Age, norms. Thus a Grade-score of 4·5

[1] This is explained more fully in Chapter Seven (cf. Fig. 6, p. 108). Any test score can be converted to a sigma score by expressing it as a deviation from the mean, and dividing by the Standard Deviation. A standard score provides a more convenient transformation by multiplying sigma scores by some conventional figure, e.g. 15, and taking a conventional mean, e.g. 100.

means that the pupil scores half-way between representative 4th Grade and 5th Grade pupils. It would be equivalent to an Educational Age (by American standards) of approximately 10·0 years. But the great majority of modern tests employ the percentile, or standard score, systems or some derivative thereof.

Chapter Four

INDIVIDUAL INTELLIGENCE TESTS

THE TERMAN-MERRILL SCALE

TERMAN and Merrill's 1937 Revision of the Stanford-Binet scale is the most extensive, and the most convenient, test for assessing the intelligence of individual children. The two forms, L and M, are both applicable from about 2 years up to superior adult level (Mental Ages 1:7 to 22:10), though they show considerable weaknesses at the top end. Form M is generally reserved for re-testing. The items are grouped under successive age-levels (usually half a dozen at each level): 2, $2\frac{1}{2}$, 3, $3\frac{1}{2}$, 4, $4\frac{1}{2}$, then by years from 5 to 14, and finally four increasingly difficult adult levels. Thus at the pre-school level each item carries one month's credit of Mental Age, from 5 to 14 two months each, and at the top end up to 6 months each. As explained in Chapter One, no testee is given the whole scale, only those levels appropriate to his ability. First the tester finds the year level at which all six items are done correctly (the basal M.A.); then testing is continued until a level is reached at which none, or only one, can be answered. Testing normally occupies anything from 30 minutes for a co-operative 7-year old to 75 minutes for a resentful adolescent; but the time also depends largely on the experience of the tester and his familiarity with the instructions and scoring, which he should know practically by heart.

At each level, four of the six items are starred for use as an abbre-viated scale. But this practice is not recommended in Britain, as the starred tests are not necessarily the most reliable. There are a number of other ways in which the skilled tester saves his own time and avoids fatiguing the child. Thus the Picture Vocabulary test provides a score at several levels from 2 to 4, according to the numbers of pictures identified; similarly the Vocabulary list of 45 graded words provides a score at 6, 8, 10 . . . and all adult levels. If, then, one of these tests is given first, not only can several credits or fails be marked off, but also the tester can fairly readily identify the basal age. Certain other tests (such as Identification by Use, Designs, etc.) appear at two or more positions in the scale, with different passing standards, and can thus be scored for all positions at one time. Many other items have three or more parts of which only two, say, have to be done correctly for a credit; thus it is seldom necessary to give the third part. Some testers jump about the scale; for example, giving all the Digit Memory, or other related groups of items, at one go. This has the additional advantage that all the most difficult and fatiguing items do not need to be applied at the end. Terman discourages this practice; however, it has been shown to have no effect on the I.Q.s of normal children, though it helps unstable ones slightly. We would therefore consider it legitimate.

For M.A.s of $4\frac{1}{2}$ upwards, the tester requires the handbook, *Measuring Intelligence* (1937), a set of printed cards, record forms, some special beads,[1] also some blocks, pennies, paper, pencil, scissors and a watch with a seconds hand. For lower M.A.s, an expensive set of standard toy objects and other practical materials is needed.[1] Though the instructions for giving and scoring each item are set out more explicitly for this test than for any other, it is particularly necessary that the tester should be thoroughly trained and experienced in their application.

The published British version of the scale has been partially, but incompletely, adapted from the American. British testers are advised to copy into their handbooks the revisions suggested by the Scottish Council for Research in Education (Kennedy Fraser, 1945).[2] As this booklet shows, the order of difficulty of many of the items is often inappropriate for British children (and the same is true of the words in the vocabulary list). In consequence, the 'scatter' of any child's performance—from his basal age up to the age of complete failure—is apt to be rather large, often as much as 6 years. Note that this scatter does *not*, as is sometimes supposed, give any indication of the testee's emotional instability.

For testees of 16 and over M.A.s are divided by 15 to give the I.Q. But the gradual deceleration of mental growth between 13 and 16 is allowed for by using 13:2 as divisor for testees aged 13:3 13:4 for those aged 13:6, and so on up to 15:0 for those aged 16:0. This device is incorporated in the C.A.-M.A.-I.Q. tables at the end of the book.

[1] These are published in Britain by Harrap.

[2] Another English revision has been prepared by Burt, but the only part of this published is his changed order of test items (Burt, 1955a).

The main types of items in Form L are shown in Table I, together with the numbers of times they occur within certain age limits.

It will be seen how largely verbal is the scale, particularly at the top end. Though toys and pictures are frequently used, especially with younger children, the responses to these as well as the instructions mostly involve the use and understanding of language.

TABLE I

CLASSIFICATION OF TERMAN-MERRILL ITEMS AT VARIOUS AGE LEVELS

	Ages				Total
	2–4½	5–9	10–14	Ad.	
Practical ingenuity with formboards, blocks	6	3	1		10
Following simple instructions . . .	3				3
Spatial: copying, drawing, reproducing designs	4	6	3	1	14
Identifying and naming objects or pictures	14				14
Vocabulary: defining concrete or abstract words; word fluency; differences between words	2	3	7	5	17
Word-relations: analogies, rhymes, similarities, sentence completion . . .	1	4	3	6	14
Pictorial relations	3	1			4
Comprehension: seeing absurdities, interpreting stories or proverbs . .	2	4	4	4	14
Pictorial comprehension	1	2	3		6
Reasoning problems			2	3	5
Counting and number problems . .		3	2	3	8
Immediate memory for digits, words or sentences	4	5	5	4	18
Memory for objects or pictures .	2				2
	42	31	30	26	129

Thus the scale penalises testees from poor cultural backgrounds or those with linguistic handicaps. On the other hand, informational items such as giving one's age, naming colours and months of the year, which figured prominently in earlier scales, have almost disappeared. The form and content of the most difficult items is appropriate enough for very bright children, but is decidedly artificial and childish for adults. Hence, even apart from the doubtful standardisation of the Terman-Merrill at the top end, most testers prefer the Wechsler scales for older children and adults.

Our Table also brings out the heterogeneous content of the scale at different levels. Although the authors have shown that every item correlates with the test as a whole, and though factor analysis yields a very large general factor (presumably $g + v$), numerous minor factors—number, space, rote memory, etc., enter to varying degrees at different ages (cf. McNemar, 1942). At the same time there are insufficient of these more specialised items to justify any differential diagnosis: for example, one cannot safely judge that a child is better on the practical than the verbal side, or strong in rote memory, and so forth. But though the only reliable outcome of the scale is a single I.Q., the individual testing situation, the diversity of items, and the fact that all responses are creative, do provide valuable opportunities for qualitative observation of how the child's mind is working and how he reacts to difficult or frustrating tasks. Thus the experienced tester can learn much of value about the child's personality and mentality, though he should also be very wary of the reliability of his 'intuitions', and realise that the child's reactions may not always be typical of his behaviour and thinking outside the testing situation.

The scale was very carefully standardised on representative American populations at each age, but nevertheless seems to be decidedly inaccurate in this country from about 11 years onwards. British testers constantly find abnormally high I.Q.s among adolescents.[1] The present writer obtains more reasonable results by counting each year of M.A. above 7:0 as 10 months. But according to Fraser Roberts and Mellone (1952), these exaggerated I.Q.s arise, not because the scale is too easy all round but because of variations in the Standard Deviation of I.Q.s at different age levels (cf. p. 105). These authors publish a useful table of corrections, based on their own findings and on the variations admitted by Terman and McNemar. Testers would do well to use these, but to ensure that the original as well as the corrected I.Q. is quoted.

---

[1] In the representative Scottish sample tested at 11 years, there were 3 per cent of I.Q.s below 70, but 10 per cent over 130 (Scottish Council for Research in Education, 1949).

It is likely that a new version of Terman-Merrill will be published shortly, combining the best items from Forms L and M, which will also attempt to overcome these irregularities.

The reliability of the scale is high, especially among duller children and older testees, less so among young bright children. Discounting the slight practice effect when Form M is given after Form L, the mean I.Q. change is about $2\frac{1}{2}$ points with I.Q.s below 70, but as much as 6 points with I.Q.s above 130. These figures correspond to an overall reliability quotient of 0·92.

In conclusion: the Terman-Merrill scale has several defects— unsuitability for adolescents and adults, differing factorial content at different age levels, unsatisfactory scoring in terms of Mental Ages and I.Q.s, and lack of restandardisation for British children.[1] Yet it continues to serve admirably most of the practical purposes of child and educational guidance.

THE WECHSLER ADULT INTELLIGENCE SCALES

The Wechsler-Bellevue scales are the accepted instruments for individual testing of adults, as is the Terman-Merrill for children, and they are similarly administered. However, they show many important differences.

(a) They are point, not age, scales. Both Forms I and II and WAIS (Wechsler Adult Intelligence Scale) contain 11 sub-tests, each covering the whole range of ability and yielding equivalent scores from 0 to 17 (0–19 in WAIS). The testee's total score is then converted directly to an I.Q., without bringing in Mental Ages. Thus every testee starts at the beginning of each sub-test and goes as far as he can. While the burden both on tester and testee of continually switching to new tasks is reduced, there is still ample opportunity for qualitative observations of the testee's temperamental reactions, or of abnormal responses to particular items.

(b) The make-up of the battery also means that the content of the test as a whole at different intelligence levels is considerably more uniform than that of the Terman-Merrill. At the same time, Wechsler's choice of sub-tests is quite arbitrary, and the perform-

---

[1] A more critical view was expressed by a Working Party of the British Psychological Society on mental deficiency in 1958, namely that the test "would now seem to be appropriate only for very young children, or (after correction for obvious sources of error) for children whose cultural background has been normal, or for those adults below high-grade imbecile level".

ance ones in particular do not provide a very representative sampling of non-verbal thinking.

(c) The test material is chosen to interest adults rather than children.

(d) Scores on the 5 (or 6) verbal and 5 non-verbal or performance sub-tests are also totalled separately to yield verbal and performance I.Q.s. While the verbal I.Q. alone gives a better indication of scholastic aptitude, Wechsler regards the Full-Scale I.Q. as providing a fairer picture of all-round intelligence in everyday life, and therefore as more appropriate for the assessment of mental defect or for other clinical purposes (there is some experimental confirmation of this claim).

(e) Both Verbal, Performance and Full-Scale I.Q.s are arranged to have the same Standard Deviation, close to 15, at all ages. However, the range of items is more restricted so that the tests do not discriminate quite as effectively as does the Terman-Merrill either within the very bright or within the mentally defective categories.[1]

(f) Separate norms are provided at each of the following age levels: 10, $10\frac{1}{4}$, $10\frac{1}{2}$, . . . $14\frac{1}{4}$, $14\frac{1}{2}$, 15, 16, 17–19, 20–24, 25–29, 30–34, . . . 55–59 years. A marked decline with age above 24 occurs on several of the sub-tests and on the total scores. But as the average I.Q. is fixed at 100 at all ages, this means that older persons are accorded higher I.Q.s than they are by other tests (such as Terman-Merrill or group tests) which make no age allowance.[2]

However, if desired, older adults can be assessed against the highest (20–24 year) norms, and the resulting quotients, which *do* decline with age, are termed Efficiency Quotients instead of Intelligence Quotients. For instance, the average 55–59 year total score is much the same as that of $11\frac{1}{2}$-year olds, and is assigned an Efficiency Quotient of 83.

(g) One or two of the sub-tests can be omitted if they appear

[1] The WAIS and WISC I.Q. norms were derived in much the same way as that described on p. 50, and therefore yield some 2 per cent of I.Q.s above 130 and below 70. But the Wechsler-Bellevue was standardised in a more roundabout manner, yielding a decidedly skewed I.Q. distribution, with only 1 per cent over 130.

[2] Mundy and Maxwell (1958) show that, among feebleminded patients, the mean Terman-Merrill I.Q. is about 10 points lower than the Wechsler at age 16–20, rising to 20 or more points at age 50–60.

inappropriate, or if time is short, but Wechsler recommends that not less than 8 should be given. The I.Q. norms are based on 5 verbal and 5 performance tests; with more or less than this the totals are corrected by an appropriate figure. The sub-tests can be given in any order that the tester likes.

As the Full Scale generally takes about an hour, many other psychologists have tried out abbreviated versions. The most popular of these is Vocabulary, Information, Similarities and Block Design. British Army and Navy psychologists during the war often used Comprehension, Vocabulary and Block Design. The results of such short scales correlate highly with the Full Scale, but are naturally less reliable, and they are not properly standardised.

(h) When the results on the 11 sub-tests are expressed as equivalent or 'weighted' scores, they are all directly comparable. Hence special strengths and weaknesses on one or more sub-tests can be observed. Similarly the Verbal and Performance I.Q.s, or the total scores on tests that do and do not hold up with age (cf. p. 172) can be contrasted. Distinctive patterns or profiles of scores are claimed to be diagnostic of different clinical conditions—mental defect, schizophrenia, neuroses, organic psychoses, etc. Probably the skilled clinical psychologist can interpret such patterns, together with qualitative features of particular responses, and thus make a valuable contribution to the differential diagnosis of mental patients (cf. Patterson, 1953). But numerous investigations have shown that the statistical reliability of separate sub-tests and of the patterns they yield is much too low for any mechanical diagnostic system. The scale is doing very well in providing Verbal and Performance I.Q.s and Efficiency Quotients, and should not be expected to yield a more detailed quantification of the testee's mentality.

There follows a list of the sub-tests. In giving the verbal tests only the Manual is needed, but the performance tests require the standard materials.[1] A variety of British translations of Americanisms have been adopted, but the British Psychological Society has now prepared a standard list.

1. General information: 25 questions covering everyday rather than specialised general knowledge.

[1] These are published by the Psychological Corporation of New York and, in Britain, by the National Foundation for Educational Research.

2. Comprehension: 10 questions involving commonsense or practical judgment; scored 2, 1 for weak answers, or 0.

3. Arithmetic problems: 10 problems to be done mentally in 15 seconds to 2 minutes each.

4. Repeating digits forwards and backwards: 14 series, ranging from 2 to 9 digits, two chances at each series.

5. Similarities: 12 questions—in what way are so-and-so alike? Scored 2, 1 or 0 for quality of generalisation.

6. Vocabulary: 42 words; scored 1, $\frac{1}{2}$ or 0.

Lists of acceptable and failing responses to most of these tests are provided.

7. Picture completion: 15 pictures in each of which some missing part has to be named; 15 seconds each.

8. Picture arrangement: 6 series consisting of 3 to 6 pictures; each series has to be arranged in the right order to tell a story, in given time-limits, and bonus marks are given for more rapid performance.

9. Object assembly: a set of 3 simple jigsaws representing a manikin, a profile and a hand; scored for pieces correct and time.

10. Block design: 9 red and white designs similar to those originally constructed by Kohs (1923), to be copied with 4, 9 or 16 coloured blocks; scored by number correct in given times, with credit for fast performance.

11. Digit-symbol substitution: a key shows 9 simple symbols paired with the numbers 1–9. Below is a mixed list of numbers, and the testee writes the corresponding symbols as quickly as possible; $1\frac{1}{2}$ minutes.

The WAIS test is more recent and is in many respects technically superior to Forms I and II. Several of the sub-tests are longer than has been indicated above. It provides norms for age-groups 16–17, 18–19, 20–24, 25–34, 35–44, 45–54, 55–64, and these have been extended (though on less thorough samples) to over 75 years.

Repetition of Form I within about a month gives retest rises of about 4 points (verbal) and 9 points (performance). The retest reliability coefficients of the Verbal and Full Scales are similar to that of Terman-Merrill, that of the Performance Scale rather lower. A typical correlation between Verbal and Performance I.Q.s is 0·71, and the median discrepancy 9 points of I.Q.; but occasional testees may differ up to 30 or 40 points in their two I.Q.s.

The Verbal Scale probably gives no better indication of educational capacities among normal adolescents and adults than a thorough group test, but has the advantage of better control of testing conditions in abnormal cases. Performance I.Q.s may be slightly more relevant than Verbal to daily life and manual occupations, but should not be interpreted as showing all-round practical ability without further evidence. The group factors measured by the various sub-tests are highly complex, but the Full Scale may be accepted as a good g test, the Verbal as mainly $g + v$.

WISC: WECHSLER INTELLIGENCE SCALE FOR CHILDREN

This is a downward extension of the previous scales, providing Verbal, Performance and Full-Scale I.Q.s over 5:0–15:11 years. Equivalent 'scaled' scores for each sub-test are listed at four-month intervals throughout. Most of the material is identical with that in Form II, the main differences being:

(a) Digit span is either omitted from the Verbal Scale, or used as an alternative.

(b) An alternative to the Digit-symbol performance test is a series of Mazes (similar to those of Porteus, p. 69). These are scored for time and errors.

(c) No Efficiency Quotients are needed, as the scale is not intended for adults.

The test is probably better standardised than any other individual scale in America, and there is no reason to suppose that this standardisation would be seriously at fault in Britain.[1] The I.Q.s are closely comparable to those of Stanford-Binet and Moray House tests, but are much more restricted at the top and bottom ends than those given by Terman-Merrill. The scale is weakest with younger, below-average children; indeed, it does not register at all at a level equivalent to 4-year M.A. and below on a Binet scale.

As in the adult scales, the Verbal and Full-Scale reliabilities are high, but the separate sub-test coefficients are too low to justify diagnosis of specialised abilities. It would seem to the writer that in most respects this scale is preferable to Terman-Merrill. Its main drawbacks are the expense of the performance material, and the rather greater amount of time that it takes to apply.

[1] The Manual and performance material are supplied by the National Foundation for Educational Research, with standard modifications for British use.

C. W. VALENTINE'S INTELLIGENCE TESTS FOR
YOUNG CHILDREN

This scale is designed specifically to help junior, infant and nursery school teachers to do their own testing. The component items are mostly very straightforward, and require no apparatus beyond the pictures given in the Manual (Valentine, 1948), or simple objects that can be prepared at home. Its cheapness is a considerable recommendation. How far teachers can be trusted to give it properly, unless they have had some training, is more doubtful. Directions for giving and scoring should be adequate, though they are less full than for Terman-Merrill.

The items are mostly assembled from other tests—Terman-Merrill, Gesell Schedules, Porteus Mazes, Burt's Reasoning Tests, etc., with a few additions. Either 8 or 10 items are provided at each age level: $1\frac{1}{2}$, 2, $2\frac{1}{2}$, 3, $3\frac{1}{2}$, 4, 5, 6, 7, 8; 6 for each year from 9 to 13 and 5 for years 14 and 15. Thus the test is suitable for children of ages 2 to 11 or 12. Though there are more items for younger children than in Terman-Merrill, it usually takes no

TABLE II

CLASSIFICATION OF ITEMS IN VALENTINE'S INTELLIGENCE TEST

	Ages		
	$1\frac{1}{2}$–4	5–9	10–15
Motor development, walking, scribbling, etc.	7	0	0
Practical ingenuity and manipulation	10	1	2
Spatial and drawing (including mazes)	3	6	7
Following simple commands	3	1	0
Vocabulary and word fluency	10	3	1
Identifying objects and pictures by name	7	0	0
Word relations	0	7	5
Picture relations	5	0	0
Comprehension—verbal	1	2	4
Comprehension—pictorial	0	4	0
Reasoning	0	6	11
Numerical	2	2	0
Immediate memory, words and digits	4	8	4
	52	40	34

longer to give since they are arranged in better order of difficulty. Nevertheless, the author recommends that testing be spread out over two or more sessions if there are signs of fatigue. Two or three items at each level are starred, but these are not to be used as an abbreviated scale; instead they are given first in order to indicate the range over which all items must be applied. With different numbers of items at different levels the scoring of Mental Age is a little complicated, but follows the same plan as in Terman-Merrill.

The items appear to be well-balanced and varied for younger children, but are somewhat more restricted than those of Terman-Merrill or WISC from about 7 on. Using a similar classification to that of Table I, the numbers of items of different types are shown above. There is no information on the factor-content of the test, but Wakelam (1944) shows that it possesses good retest reliability, and gives useful predictions of educability among backward juniors. Unfortunately there is no information, either, regarding the Standard Deviation of I.Q.s at different age levels: hence it is not possible to say whether a high or a low result represents the same degree of superiority or inferiority throughout.

INFANT TESTS: GRIFFITHS'S MENTAL DEVELOPMENT SCALE

There are several American pre-school scales, such as the Merrill-Palmer and Minnesota, which—being based on play materials—are particularly attractive to 2- to 5-year olds (cf. Anastasi, 1954). But they are not described here because of the difficulties in procuring the materials.

One may ask whether there is any point in testing children younger than 3 or 4 years. The results are likely to be very misleading if they are regarded as predictive of later intelligence. Moreover, it is far more difficult to set up standard testing conditions for babies; they are highly distractible, easily fatigued, variable from day to day, upset by strange surroundings or an unfamiliar tester, and their responses are often so indefinite or ambiguous that the tester has to use his personal judgment in scoring them. Nevertheless, psychologists such as Gesell, Valentine, Bayley and Griffiths rightly point out that the young child's motor, sensory, language and social reactions tend to develop in a very regular order, and do so at different rates in different individuals. These functions are basic to the later development of intellectual abilities, and even if a single testing has little diagnostic value, it is often revealing to trace a child's progress throughout the pre-school period. Moreover, it is of great importance to be able, at an early age, to recognise serious retardation in, say, co-ordination or hearing, which may indicate pathological conditions.

The best known scale for infants—Gesell's Developmental Schedules—makes no claim to measure intelligence or even to give an all-round growth quotient (Gesell and Amatruda, 1947). These schedules provide norms or standards of development for 4, 18, 28 and 40 weeks and 12, 18, 24 and 36 months in four main areas: bodily co-ordination, eye-hand co-ordination, speech, and personal-social behaviour. Bühler and Hetzer's (1935) more elaborate series of tests are scored to give a developmental quotient, and P. Cattell's set of infant tests (1940) is designed to connect up with the bottom end of the Terman-Merrill scale. Griffiths's scale (1954), which we shall describe here, is not only the most accessible in Britain, but is also probably the most comprehensive and best standardised of any. It contains 3 items per week for the first year of life, and 2 for the second year, that is, 260 in all. They are grouped under five headings, scores on which are practically equivalent throughout, so that the scale yields a profile of development under each heading as well as an overall result called the G.Q. or General Quotient. The headings, together with specimen items for babies a few weeks old and for children approaching 2 years, are as follows:

	Soon after birth	*Approaching 2 years*
A. Locomotor	Kicking, head-lifting	Walking downstairs unaided
B. Personal-social	Smiling, recognition of mother	Asking for things at table
C. Hearing-speech	Startled by noises	Uses sentences of 4+ syllables
D. Eye and hand	Following moving lights	Throwing ball into basket
E. Performance	Grasping objects	Assembling parts of a toy

Other items are based on standard toy apparatus,[1] and several of them are filled in from general observation or from information given by the mother. The time taken for testing is usually under 30 minutes. As in the Binet, tests are given from a point on the scale where there are 6 successive passes up to a point where there are 6 successive fails. But the scores are expressed in weeks, and divided by weeks of age to yield quotients. The Standard Deviation of G.Q.s is close to 12 at all ages, so that quotients seldom exceed 135 or fall below 65. This unusually narrow range would be expected, because of the very heterogeneous content of the scale (cf. p. 107). The standardisation appears adequate, and good reliability (when applied by a skilled tester) is shown by a correlation of 0·92 for 52 children retested after a mean interval of 30 weeks.[2] Reliabilities for the five sub-scales are not given; they would certainly be lower. Their overlapping is probably high, hence differential diagnosis from the profile must be made with great caution. There is no information regarding future predictive value, but from the results of American scales we would expect virtually no correlation between a single testing in the first year and intelligence at 5 years or later. Finally, we should re-emphasise that the application of tests at this level necessitates exceptional skill in handling babies and training in giving and scoring the items.

PERFORMANCE TESTS: COLLINS–DREVER SCALE

Performance tests based on jigsaw puzzles, manipulations of blocks, or drawings are naturally attractive to children. Thus they are useful in establishing good rapport at the beginning of a—largely oral—Terman-Merrill session, even if their results are of poor diagnostic value. And they provide excellent opportunities for observing temperamental reactions to difficulties. But they are mostly unwieldy and very costly. And they are so dependent on specific abilities, and affected by chance factors of unreliability, that a considerable number must be given for a trustworthy M.A. or I.Q. Even then it is doubtful what the result represents, apart from providing a check on, or helping to correct some bias in, a more verbal test. Thus a child with language handicaps, and many delinquents with defective schooling, tend to score higher on performance tests; whereas children with a greater oral facility,

[1] Supplied by the author.
[2] Later work by other testers has yielded far less favourable figures.

and some nervous ones who prefer academic to practical activities, do relatively poorly. Another weakness in performance tests is the large practice effect; scores tend to rise markedly on retesting even after two years.

When a miscellaneous set of tests is given, as in the original Pintner-Paterson scale, each test has its own M.A. norms, and the median of these Mental Ages is usually taken as the final score. The trouble with this is that several of the component tests may be poorly standardised. More accurate norms are generally available for such point scales as Wechsler's and Arthur's (another American series), and Collins and Drever's. Here, so many points are awarded for varying degrees of success on each test, and the total points are converted to an M.A. or I.Q. by a single set of norms. This means that the whole battery, lasting perhaps a full hour, must always be given; the other system allows more flexibility.

The Collins-Drever scale was originally devised for testing deaf children (Drever and Collins, 1936).[1] It was found that they score as highly as hearing children on this type of test, though about 3 M.A. years inferior to the average on verbal tests. The scale can be given with oral or with pantomime directions.

Scale A contains 11 sub-tests:

1. Kohs Block Design: from 4 to 16 coloured blocks are provided which have to be arranged so as to reproduce a series of 10 patterns; 2 to 4 points are given for each pattern completed in a set time.

2. Knox Cubes: reproduction of patterns tapped out on 4 cubes. These range from 1, 2, 3, 4 to 1, 3, 4, 2, 1, 2.

3. Dominoes: another memory span test; picking out up to 6 dominoes in correct order from a set numbered 0 to 10.

4. Arranging 5 cubes by size and 5 brass weights by weight in correct order.

5. Manikin puzzle: pieces correct in time limit.

6. Feature profile: ditto.

7. Two-figure Formboard: 9 rectangular or triangular pieces to be fitted into 2 frames; scored by time.

8. Healy Puzzle A: 5 rectangular pieces to be fitted in a frame.

9. Cube Construction: 3 large wooden blocks painted on certain sides; 8 or 9 small cubes to be put together to reproduce these

---

[1] Material supplied by Baird Scientific Instrument Co., Edinburgh.

models; scored by number of cubes correctly assembled in 5 minutes each.

10. Star Picture: a picture of Little Bopeep from which 12 sections have been cut to be reinserted; scored by number in given time.

11. Healy Picture Completion I: a large picture with 10 square holes, to be filled by choosing among 50 square pieces; scored by number and aptness of choices in 5 minutes.

Median total scores and quartiles are listed for boys and girls aged $5\frac{1}{2}$ to $15\frac{1}{2}$, girls being 1 to 2 years behind boys throughout. If scores are thus expressed as M.A.s and then divided by C.A. in the usual way, the resulting I.Q.s are not comparable with Binet or Wechsler I.Q.s, having a Standard Deviation of about 25. Hence a separate table of deviation I.Q. norms is provided, as for the Moray House tests. Tentative M.A. norms are given also for an abbreviated scale consisting of Kohs, Cube Construction and Healy Picture Completion I. I.Q.s obtained from this will certainly have an abnormally wide spread.

Scale B, consisting of 7 tests, is recommended for younger children. Tentative 4-to-7 year M.A. norms are given.

1. Sizes and weights as in Scale A.

2. Manikin: ditto.

3. Knox Cubes: a simpler series of patterns.

4. Seguin-Goddard Formboard (cf. p. 70); scored by time for correct completion.

5. Dearborn Triangle Formboard: number of pieces filled in 5 minutes.

6. Mare and Foal: a picture test with missing pieces to be inserted in given time.

7. Teacher and Class: ditto.

W. P. ALEXANDER'S PERFORMANCE TEST SCALE

The three tests which constitute this scale were shown, by factorial research, to involve a considerable practical or spatial ability factor in addition to their g-content. Thus they are regarded as particularly suitable for selection for technical education. Alexander (1935) states that they measure "capacity to think in a concrete situation".[1]

Kohs Blocks and Cube Construction use the same material and

[1] Materials and Manual supplied by Nelsons.

are given in the same manner as in the Collins-Drever scale. But in order to improve their discrimination a more elaborate scoring system is introduced, allotting so many points for success at the various models and for time taken. The third test is a new one, Passalong, consisting of nine boxes each containing one red and several blue squares or rectangles. By sliding the pieces around, the red block has to be moved from the bottom to the top position. The problems are steeply graded in difficulty, and are scored by time for each success. The three tests can be given in about 40 minutes.

The total points are translated into Mental Ages, with separate norms for boys and girls from 7 to 19. There is no appreciable increase in score beyond 15, and higher M.A.s are arbitrary. The resulting I.Q. is called P.A.R. (Practical Ability Ratio). It is said to be comparable to a Moray House or Terman-Merrill I.Q., so that a 10-points difference indicates relative suitability for technical or academic education. But actually the Standard Deviation of P.A.R.s seems to be considerably higher—over 20 at 11 years—and the norms are probably too lenient; hence it is far easier to get high P.A.R.s than verbal I.Q.s. Watts and Slater (1950) suggest therefore that local percentile or standard-score norms should be collected if the scale is used widely for allocation purposes. In the writer's view, paper-and-pencil spatial tests are preferable in such a situation. They measure much the same abilities more reliably, are more readily applied to large numbers, and are less likely to be upset by previous practice or by the handing on of information from boys who are tested early to those tested later. Alternatively, a complete revision of Kohs Blocks and Cube Construction for group application, with smaller blocks and new designs, has been constructed by Jones and Hey (1952). Norms are supplied for boys around 11 years.

SETS OF SEPARATE PERFORMANCE TESTS

None of the above scales meets the needs of testers who simply want:

(*a*) to be able to observe the testee working at practical tasks;

(*b*) to have sufficient tests to provide a fairly reliable contrast with the strongly verbal Terman-Merrill;

(*c*) to keep the time spent on such tests fairly short, and if need be, omit one or two.

The present writer would suggest the following sets, each test being scored separately, and the median or mean M.A. taken. They are *not* suitable for calculating performance I.Q.s.

A. For children with probable M.A. 10 upwards and adults:
   1. Kohs Block (Alexander or Trist-Misselbrook).
   2*a*. Porteus Mazes. 2*b*. Mazes time score.
   3. Oakley or Moorrees Formboard.
   4. (If time allows) Cube Construction.

B. For children with probable M.A. 4 to 9 years.
   1. Goddard Formboard.
   2. Porteus Mazes
   3. Goodenough Draw-a-Man.
   4. Mare and Foal and/or
   5. WISC Kohs Blocks.

Kohs Blocks. No separate age or sex norms are published except for the original—very lengthy—version. The Wechsler and WISC versions are relatively brief, and it is possible to convert the scaled score norms into Mental Ages. Another accessible version is Alexander's adaptation of the Collins-Drever sub-test. The present writer collected the tentative norms for boys which are shown in Table III below; these badly need confirmation. Girls tend to score half a year behind boys at M.A. 8·0, 1 year at 13 and $1\frac{1}{2}$ years at 17.

Quite a different version for adult recruits was developed by Trist and Misselbrook during World War II, and is described by Semeonoff and Trist (1958).

Cube Construction. This is probably a better test than Passalong. Owing to the lack of norms for other versions, it may be given according to Gaw's procedure (1925). However, if Alexander's procedure is preferred, some very rough norms for boys are listed in Table III.

Mare and Foal. This is particularly attractive for younger children. The geometrical insets are not removed and no account is taken of errors. The writer would put fair trust in the norms tabulated below, though discrimination is obviously poor above 9·0 years. Boys may be scored half a year more strictly, and girls half a year less strictly than the figures shown here.

PORTEUS MAZES

This well-known test of 'foresight and planning capacity' dates back to 1914. It consists of a graded series of mazes through which the child has to draw a path without divagations. There is one for each year-level from 3 to 12, 1 for 14 years and 1 adult. Thus the score in M.A. years consists simply of the level of the most difficult maze accomplished, though this is complicated by allowances for errors which are corrected at second or further attempts. Neither the norms nor the reliability of the test are very satisfactory (Tizard, 1951). But Porteus presents considerable evidence for the claim that it corresponds better than most verbal tests with adaptability to the social and practical requirements of everyday life. Scores appear also to be more susceptible to brain injury and leucotomy operations.

A slightly revised series of mazes was issued in 1933, and the older series (given, for example, in Burt's *Handbook of Mental Tests*) should not be used. Porteus requires a fresh set of blanks to be used by each testee at each trial (i.e. 2 to 4 copies of any maze at which errors occur). To save expense we suggest using Valentine's version, where the one set is not marked, but traced by a dry paintbrush or pen-point.[1] In this case the tester must be most careful not to allow self-corrections; and the full instructions in Porteus's Manual (1952) should be consulted, particularly in regard to scoring the 12- and 14-year mazes.

The writer has shown that it is worth recording secretly the aggregate time spent on Mazes XI, XII and XIV among testees likely to complete all three (Vernon, 1937).[2] Recommended norms are tabulated below. Though this speed score correlates moderately with Binet M.A., it is independent of Maze score and helps to differentiate the cautious from the impulsive testee. Porteus also presents a detailed method of scoring carelessness and errors which yields a Qualitative or Q-score. This is claimed to be much higher (i.e. worse) among delinquent adolescents and adults than among normals. Though a promising technique, it fails to make adequate allowance for the level reached on the

[1] Valentine (1946) does not include the Adult maze by which the maximum score is raised from 15 to 17 M.A. years.
[2] If an error is made, stop timing and start again when the testee reaches the same position at the next trial.

FIG. 1 Seguin Form Board: Positions of Pieces in Three Heaps
Ready for Re-insertion.

test, and there is as yet little independent confirmation of its
validity (cf. Gibbens, 1958).

FORMBOARDS

For young children the Seguin or Goddard Formboard is a
remarkably effective test, certainly more dependent on intelligence than—as might be supposed—on mere manual dexterity.
Yet it is very simple, being scored by the time taken to put 10
variously shaped wooden pieces into appropriate holes in a board.
Several versions are available. We recommend the large board
with loosely fitting insets, shown in Fig. 1.[1] Three trials are allowed, and the M.A. can be determined from the average of
total-time and best-trial norms, as listed in Table III.

[1] Made by Baird Scientific Instrument Co., Edinburgh.

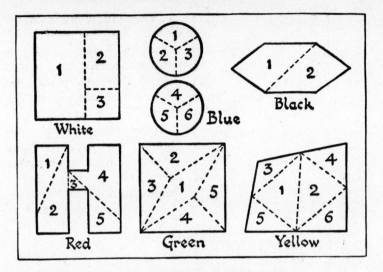

FIG. 2 Oakley Form Board.

At a more difficult level there are several choices, though unfortunately none is at present manufactured in this country. The Kent-Shakow or Worcester Formboard (clinical model) can be obtained from America (cf. Buros, 1953). The Moorrees Formboard has been described by the writer elsewhere (Vernon, 1937), and norms provided. The Oakley Formboard, shown in Fig. 2, involves arranging 2 to 6 coloured pieces in each of 7 holes. It is sufficiently complex to tax the highest levels of practical ability, and provides excellent opportunities for observing the testee's methods of work (cf. Oakley, 1935).

GOODENOUGH DRAW-A-MAN TEST

This is a particularly easy test to give, the child simply being encouraged to draw the best picture of a man that he can. The artistic quality of his product does not enter into the scoring; rather, a good score depends on accurate observation and the development of concepts of the human figure and clothing. The presence or absence of 51 specific points is noted, ranging from: Head present, legs present, to sleeves and trousers non-transparent, opposition of thumb shown, etc.

TABLE III

NORMS FOR SELECTED PERFORMANCE TESTS

Performance Test M.A.	4·0	5·0	6·0	7·0	8·0	9·0	10·0	11·0	12·0	13·0	14·0	15·0	16·0	17·0	18·0	19·0	20·0
Goddard (best of three trials)	54	40	30	24	21	18½	16½	15	14	13							
(Total of three trials)	190	140	112	91	75	66	59	53	48	44	41						
Mare and Foal (seconds)	180	100	75	59	46	38	34	31	29								
Cube Construction—																	
Alexander (points)				21	28	36	47	55	62	66	73	79	85	91	96	100	
Kohs–Alexander (points)					5	10	15	21	28	37	48	58	68	76	83	90	95
Porteus Mazes speed (seconds)						500	428	357	298	247	200	170	143	119	102	86	72

Very careful study of the scoring instructions in Goodenough's Manual (1926) is essential. Even trained scorers are apt to differ, and this factor, combined with the variability of the child's performance on different occasions, means that the reliability of the test is rather unsatisfactory. The published norms appear to apply pretty accurately to British children.

Chapter Five

GROUP INTELLIGENCE TESTS

GROUP tests have obvious advantages where large numbers of children or adults are to be tested, namely economy of time and the fact that they can be given and scored by teachers or other persons without special training. Indeed, they are perhaps too easy to get hold of, and the need for skilful handling of the testees and for training in interpretation of results is insufficiently realised.

Among older school pupils and average or above-average adults they are often more reliable and at least as valid as individual tests, since they can readily be constructed to suit the requisite range of ability; whereas individual tests are most needed at the bottom end of the scale and cannot simultaneously cover the upper ranges as thoroughly. The group test, however, implicitly assumes that all testees are in the right frame of mind, that they will co-operate and work keenly and quickly, follow the tester's oral instructions, and be capable of reading and understanding any printed instructions. But these assumptions cannot always be fulfilled, and the great advantage of the individual test is that the tester can control such disturbing factors as fatigue, poor eyesight, poor reading ability, anxiety or undue caution, distractibility and inadequate motivation. If he cannot dispel these he can at least observe their effects on test performance, which the group tester cannot. For such reasons individual tests are absolutely essential for pre-school children, and very desirable for 5–7-year olds. The proportion of unstable children who fail to settle down to the group test situation decreases with age, though even at 11 there are probably 1 or 2 per cent who do not do themselves justice (cf. Connor, 1952). All suspected defectives, psychotics, brain-damaged patients and certain types of neurotics similarly require individual handling if their results are to be meaningful.

The same holds good for educational tests. After all, children are not usually expected to cope with formal examinations till 9, 10 or later. Class exercises are often introduced earlier, but nothing vital hangs on them, and the teacher can generally observe if there are misunderstandings or disturbing influences.

At the same time we should point out that the good reliability and validity of most group tests ensures that their results cannot be so seriously affected by the testees' feelings and motivation, or by the manner in which the test is given, as some critics suppose. War-time studies of the effects of state of health, and menstruation in women, on test performance yielded entirely negative results (cf. Vernon and Parry, 1949). And some investigations of incentives suggest that when children are made extra-keen by the offering of monetary rewards, they attempt more items but also get more wrong, so that their actual scores are little altered. Nevertheless, we agree with Heim (1954) that more research is needed into the effects of the attitudes of the testees, and that there is a good case for seeing that testers are adequately trained to instil the proper atmosphere, as well as to follow the instructions.

The reading capacity of the testees requires consideration in almost all group tests. Thus it has been demonstrated that the typical intelligence test for 11-year olds requires a reading age of over 9 years for the understanding of instructions and verbal items. This means that, for the bottom quarter of the age group, such tests are effectively little more than reading tests. Many arithmetic problem tests likewise depend almost as much on reading as number capacity. Luckily the borderline for selection to grammar schools normally falls around M.A. $11\frac{1}{2}$ to $12\frac{1}{2}$. There are non-verbal tests, also orally applied verbal tests, which do not involve much, or any, reading (cf. below). These, therefore, can be applied earlier in the junior school. Naturally they make considerable demands on the clarity, accuracy and class-control of the tester and become more and more unreliable below, say, 8 years. Moreover, non-verbal test materials are of relatively little value for educational predictions simply because they involve group factors other than verbal ability.

Other reasons why most psychologists prefer to rely on an individual test when important decisions have to be taken are the greater artificiality of the new-type items of which group tests are composed, and the fact that they are almost always done at speed. This latter factor (which is discussed more fully on p. 181) should not be exaggerated, since the predictive value of suitably constructed group tests is remarkably high. But in so far as capacity for working at speed is affected by age, tests for adults who range widely in age should usually have generous time limits.

VARIETIES OF TESTS AND ITEMS

In addition to the classification—oral, printed verbal, non-verbal or mixed—tests may belong to the battery or the omnibus types. Both normally include half a dozen to a dozen kinds of items, each ranging from easy to difficult. But in the battery test all the items of any one kind are put together in a sub-test with its own instructions and practice samples, and with its own time limit (which may be anything from 3 to 20 minutes). In the omnibus test, however, all kinds of items are mixed up; or there are short sets of each kind, first at an easy, then at more difficult levels. There is a single time limit for the whole test (usually 45 minutes, though ranging from 30 to 90), which means that it is more easily applied by an untrained tester, without a stop-watch. In this form, it is more difficult to provide adequate instructions and explanations. Sometimes a preliminary practice sheet is given with examples of each kind of item, but usually each item-type has to be explained and illustrated each time it recurs; as no oral help can be given, comprehension of and attention to the printed instructions become a major part of the test. Convenience of administration also means that the testees have to work without a break. Possibly the short spells at the separate sub-tests in a battery induce better concentration. Nevertheless, no one has ever proved that omnibus tests are any less valid,[1] and it should always be remembered that, in either form, every set of items *with its instructions* has been tried out beforehand and found to work. The same answer can be given to armchair critics who complain that certain items (usually taken out of context) are far too difficult, and that children should not be expected to do 100 of them in 45 minutes. It is, of course, only the oldest and brightest children for whom the test is intended who finish, or nearly finish it. Average children are not *expected* to do 50 or so items, but have been found to do so.

We have admitted that the items commonly used are somewhat artificial. Though there are innumerable minor variations in form, and the precise content differs in every new test, yet the

---

[1] A controlled experiment by the present writer showed that there was no difference in the coach-ability or susceptibility to practice of omnibus and battery tests; also that the average scores were, if anything, slightly higher in the omnibus version.

range of thinking processes called upon is remarkably limited. It would seem as though the early psychometrists—Ebbinghaus, Spearman, Terman, Otis, Thomson and Burt—chose a few species quite arbitrarily which were easy to construct and administer and score objectively; and that few later authors have been able to escape from their conventions. Almost inevitably such items are limited to 'closed systems' of thinking (p. 39), predetermined by the test constructor, and thus may fail to include the rich varieties of thought that children and adults display in everyday life. Nevertheless if new and more natural items could be invented, it would very likely be found that they would measure the same g (or R) and V factors as the present ones. Moreover, Guilford and his colleagues are now greatly expanding the range, and attempting to show whether additional group factors are involved.

Almost all the item-species described and illustrated below can be applied to each variety of material: (a) words, (b) symbols such as letters, (c) numbers, (d) diagrams and figures, (e) pictures. Indeed, it is somewhat disconcerting to learn, from Guilford's results, that each of these seems to embody its own group factor, so that differences in abilities at different materials may even outweigh in influence differences in kinds or levels of thinking. For example, it seems to be more difficult to distinguish reasoning from verbal comprehension than reasoning-out verbal problems from non-verbal ones.

Directions Items (oral or printed)

Ex. 12. If the moon is larger than the sun, write the letter K; if not, write R.

Alternatively, testees may be directed to mark particular figures or pictures on their answer sheets. More difficult items become more complex, thus invoking a considerable effort of comprehension; or sometimes they bring in spatial orientation.

Ex. 13. Draw 6 circles, 2 large and 4 small ones, none of them touching. Two of the small circles should be inside one of the large ones, the others outside.

Vocabulary and Opposites

Ex. 14. Discord means the opposite of (contented, laughter, encouragement, harmony, comfort)

15. Underline the word which means   SHUN
     most nearly the same as the word   hate   stand
     in capital letters   avoid   destroy
                                examine   exclude

16. What is it that flies through the air, and can sing?
     (aeroplane, butterfly, music, nightingale)

Note that the wrong alternatives are chosen as being fairly plausible errors. Another variant is the synonym-antonym test (Ex. 11). Yet another takes the following form:

Ex. 17. Underline two of the following words which mean *either* the same as *or* the opposite of each other.

(quick perfunctory tardy metallic smelling meticulous upright)

General Information

Ex. 18. The tuna is a kind of: musical instrument, fish, bird, weapon.

Provided such items are drawn from a wide field rather than dependent on specialised knowledge, this test correlates very highly with other verbal intelligence tests. (Indeed, there is obviously little to distinguish Ex. 18 from Ex. 16.) However, informational items show a considerable sex difference in favour of males, whereas more purely linguistic ones tend to favour females. A variant is sometimes called the:

Always Has Test

Ex. 19. A shop always has:

        (salesmen, books, a fireplace, a door)

The same type of item can be expressed in terms of pictures, given with oral directions.

The next two species might be termed Word (or Non-verbal) Relationships.

Classification

Ex. 20. Underline the one word (figure, etc.) which does not belong with the rest—or which is the 'odd man out'.

      Table   Crate   Fireplace   Mallet   Door

Ex. 21. DCX   GHV   LKT   JIZ   FER

Ex. 22.

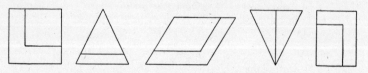

Similar tests are constructed of pictures of familiar objects. The capacity to generalise and abstract the common feature always has a high *g*-saturation. Nevertheless, it is difficult to make this item-form watertight. Thus in Ex. 20 it might be argued that Mallet (the only tool) is as good an answer as Fireplace (the only one not made of wood). The following is less ambiguous, but also more complex to 'get across'.

Ex. 23.   The three words in capitals are alike in some way. Under-line two of the other words which also belong.

IVORY SNOW MILK (water cottonwool butter cold flour)

Analogies. These have probably been more widely used than any other type. The ordinary verbal form is illustrated in Ex. 7. Pictorial or figural ones can likewise be devised at an easy or a difficult level.

Ex. 24.

A complex variant is:

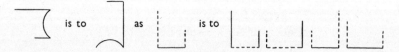

Ex. 25.   Underline two of the words in brackets which are connected in the same way as the words in capitals.

HOUR is to MINUTE as: (day second clock minute time week)

Analogies can also be expressed in matrix-form; note that the following overlap with our later category of Induction tests.

Ex. 26. Fill in the missing number

2	5	8
4	10	16
8	20	—

Ex. 27. Underline one of the four figures which fills the gap.

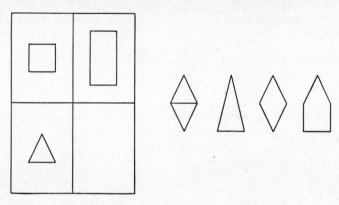

Next we have several species which might be generally termed comprehension of sentences, pictures or shapes. Ebbinghaus's Sentence Completion (Ex. 1) was the first of these. For objective marking it is almost essential to turn it into multiple-choice form.

Ex. 28. The star shines more often in the dark than in summer.

	moon		summer	winter.
	sun		winter	the night.

Almost indistinguishable items occur in Reading Comprehension tests (cf. p. 96). The same form can be used to provide a type of reasoning test.

Ex. 29. John is one year older than Peter, and Stephen is 3 years younger than John. Hence Peter is 2 years older than Stephen.

	1	last year.
	3	John.

Completion items can also be used in the pictorial medium—for example, a door with a knob missing: the testee has to draw it in, or select it from pictures of other objects. Figures or patterns provide other possibilities (cf. Exs. 27 and 55). Here is a numerical example:

Ex. 30. Fill in + or − signs between these numbers so that they give the correct answers:

$$3 \quad 2 \quad 3 = 8$$
$$11 \quad 6 \quad 8 \quad 4 = 9$$

Mixed Sentences. Re-arrangement of the words of a sentence in correct order involves grasping its sense. One way of avoiding the need for testees to rewrite the sentence is illustrated in Ex. 9. Here is another:

> Ex. 31. Underline two words which, if changed around, would make the sentence sensible.
>
> No sacrifice can be obtained without some object.

Mixed words, i.e. anagrams, are occasionally used, but probably involve a rather larger specific component than other verbal tests.

True-False and Absurdities

> Ex. 32. If tomorrow were Monday, yesterday would be Sunday. (Underline TRUE or FALSE)

> Ex. 33. ALL   SOME   NO   motor cars travel faster than railway trains.

> Ex. 34. The road from my house goes downhill all the way to town and downhill all the way home again. (Underline SILLY or SENSIBLE)

or multiple-choice answers are provided, one of which explains why the statement is absurd.

Obviously there is little distinction between these and *Information* or *Always Has* items on the one hand, and *Reasoning* items on the other. This type of item is very suitable for oral presentation, since the response involves a minimum of reading. Pictorial absurdities are likewise used.

Proverbs. This is a clumsy type of item, but it is certainly effective in eliciting comprehension of complex sentences. Usually a set of English (or foreign or imaginary) proverbs has to be matched with a set of explanations. Thus, in these examples B is the answer to Ex. 35, and A to Ex. 36.

> Ex. 35. Look before you leap.

> Ex. 36. Handsome is as handsome does.

> A. Good deeds are more important than good looks.
> B. Don't do anything important without taking care.
> C. Behave well to other people if you want them to behave well to you.

Reasoning. When the testee has to carry out mental manipulations of the material presented, put forward hypotheses, and check them, we may call it reasoning or problem-solving. Most of the item-types so far illustrated involve such reasoning when they reach a certain level of difficulty; but the following are more direct examples.

Ex. 37. Margaret is shorter than Kathleen, and Kathleen is taller than Joan. Who is the tallest? (Margaret Kathleen Joan Can't tell).

Ex. 38. In a class of 30 children, 20 were boys and 10 were girls. Half the class played cricket and the other half played hockey. Did any boys play hockey? (Yes No Can't Say)

More complex examples may employ formal logical syllogisms, as in Valentine's series for superior adults (1954), or may be elaborated into something resembling a short detective story. Other problems may be based on spatial orientation.

Ex. 39. A man started walking west; he turned right, then right again, then left. In what direction was he walking now?

Ordinary problem arithmetic sums also often appear in intelligence tests, and are known to provide one of the best tests of R (reasoning).

It is difficult to find agreement among factorists as to how many reasoning factors should be distinguished, or whether they can all be reduced to Spearman's g. Nevertheless there is considerable evidence for separating deductive reasoning from inductive. The former involves thinking out the logical consequences of given premises (as in Exs. 37 and 38), whereas the latter depends on the discovery of an underlying principle (as in Exs. 46 to 55). On the other hand, the difference may be merely that deduction tests are almost always verbal, whereas induction ones are usually figural, symbolic or numerical. Other tests which tend to fall under the deductive heading are Pedigrees, Codes or Substitution, and Language translations.

In *Pedigrees*, a complex chart of 3 or more generations of a family is shown and several questions asked on it of the kind:

Ex. 40. What relation is John to William? (brother cousin uncle stepbrother brother-in-law)

Codes take various forms:

Ex. 41. A boy made up a code in which LONDON was written JMLBML. What did the code letters UCCI stand for?

(This would appear to be as much inductive as deductive.)

Ex. 42. In another code, A = 2, B = 4, C = 6, D = 8, E = 10, etc. What is the code for Z?

Ex. 43. In the same code, if you subtract C from F and add B, what *letter* would be the answer?

Digit-Symbol Substitution is another simple type of coding.

Ex. 44.

Write the correct number under each symbol, doing as many as possible in 2 minutes.

Possibly this should be classified as a perceptual speed test, but it has been included in several non-verbal intelligence tests (cf. p. 59).

Translations

Ex. 45. The Sanskrit sentence:

KAMALA MONOHARAM means, in English, 'A lovely lotus'.
TADAGE VARTATI KAMALAM means, in English, 'The lotus is in the pond'.

What is the Sanskrit word for 'lotus' ...?
What is the Sanskrit word for 'lovely' ...?

Induction Tests. The most widely used of these is the *Number Series* (cf. Ex. 8). The same principle can be embodied in *Letter Series* and *Figure Series*.

Ex. 46. b a d c f e ... Write, or underline, the letter that comes next (f g h i).

Ex. 47.

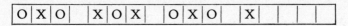

Continue the pattern.

Ex. 48.

Underline one of these which would fill the gap.

Ex. 49.

These five figures could be re-arranged in a series; underline the middle one of the series.

The same item-forms can be used with pictures (e.g. stages in a boy's getting up and going to school), or—less readily—with words.

Ex. 50. Summer   New Year   Easter   Christmas   November (Underline the middle item, or the first and last items).

The *Abstraction* item-form, introduced by Shipley (1940), is particularly appropriate for symbolic materials. It can also cover analogies, codes and other problems with the same very simple set of instructions:

Wherever you see an asterisk, one letter or number is missing; write in the missing letters or numbers.

Ex. 51. 3 7 6 4   4 3 7 6   6 4 3 7   * * * *

52. luck lick lack   foul foil   * * * *

53. quay key owe oh son   * * *

54. England 1234526   France 785291   Greece * * * * * *

Finally we have the complex two-dimensional series item, as represented by Raven's Progressive Matrices test.

Ex. 55.

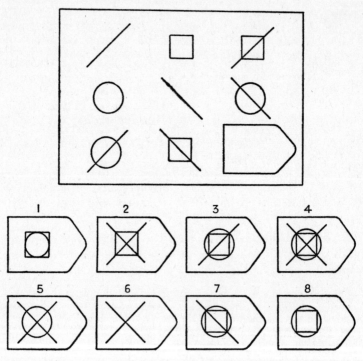

FIG. 3 Specimen Item as in the Progressive Matrices Test. Which of the Numbered Pieces 1–8, if fitted into the empty space above, would complete the pattern?

TESTS INVOLVING OTHER FACTORS

All the above items can be regarded chiefly as measures of g and V, though some factor analysts would classify several of them under various reasoning factors. Those to be mentioned now may also be found in published intelligence tests, but tend to show clearer evidence of distinctive factors, particularly among relatively homogeneous groups, such as grammar school pupils or university students.

N or *number factor* is evident in any numerical material (e.g.

Number Series), but chiefly occurs in simple Four Rules sums which have much lower g or V saturations.

k or *S* tests. *Spatial factors* do not necessarily play a large part in all tests based on figural materials, nor in orientation problems (Ex. 39). Many testees, for example, may solve Matrices items largely by verbal, logical reasoning. It is the mental manipulation of shapes, or visualising them as turned around, recombined, etc., that seems to be the essence of *k*. Three examples, the Paper Formboard, 'Squares' and 'Figure Construction' are illustrated by Vernon and Parry (1949). Another follows:

Ex. 56. Which of these four is the same as the first shape turned around?

57. Which is the same as the first shape turned over, or as seen in a mirror?

58. Which is the same as the first shape turned over *and* around?

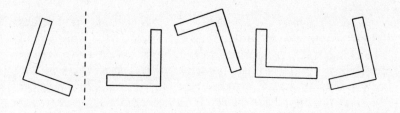

Block-counting was used in Army Beta, the American Army General Classification Test of World War II, and other batteries.

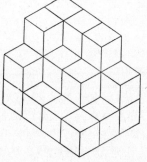

Ex. 59. Count the total number of blocks in the pile, including those you cannot see.

60. How many blocks in the pile touch at least 5 other blocks full face?

Perceptual Speed or Clerical Factor. When the testee is merely required to make comparisons at speed and pick out a shape, word or number which is identical with the initial one, a somewhat different factor enters. The *g*-saturation is considerably reduced, and such tests correlate well with capacity for clerical work. The more general problem of the speed factor in intelligence tests is discussed later (p. 181).

Fluency Tests. These are supposed to measure speed and richness of mental associations rather than understanding of ideas, though in fact they overlap rather closely with vocabulary and other *V* tests in unselected groups (cf. Rogers, 1953).

Ex. 61. Write down as many names of birds (flowers, etc.) as you can in 3 minutes.

62. Write down words beginning with F, or ending in -tion, etc.

Other fluency tests are based on associations with inkblots or pictures.

Flexibility-rigidity in the Formation of New Concepts. Luchins (1947) has proposed certain tests in which a standard 'set', or method of tackling a series of problems, is established; then a new type of problem is introduced, and the tendency to perseverate with the standard method gives a measure of *in*flexibility. This construct plays an important part in psychopathological work where, for example, it is claimed that brain-injured, senile or some psychotic patients are differentiated from normals more by their inability to form new concepts than by low intelligence as conventionally tested. Similarities or classification tests (particularly non-verbal), Kohs Blocks, and Proverbs have shown some value in this context, and Wechsler denotes several sub-tests in his scale as deteriorating strongly with age (cf. p. 172). Similarly, Shipley (1940) contrasted Abstraction with Vocabulary items. It is not yet clear whether this distinction amounts to anything more than the distinction between *g* and *v* factors. Also it is doubtful whether the Luchins type of test brings in any new ability. However, a concept-formation factor has been demonstrated by Lovell (1955) in non-verbal classification and in what are called sorting tests.

Ex. 63. Sort these pieces into three boxes so that in each box the pieces are all of the same kind.

	Nos. of pieces	Description of Category
Box. 1.	....	....
Box. 2.	....	....
Box. 3.	....	....

Now sort the pieces again into three boxes, but in a different way.

Box. 4.	....	....
etc.		

Creativity and Originality. An early form of test consisted of such questions as:

Ex. 64. If everyone in the world suddenly went blind, write out as many consequences as possible that would be likely to occur in our modes of living.

These are difficult to score; but by compiling a list of all the suggestions put forward by a large number of testees it is possible to mark any subsequent set of answers objectively for cleverness and unusualness. Guilford has devised several other such tests which yield a distinctive factor, and which appear to predict aptitude for creative work (cf. Wilson, 1954). These include thinking of unusual uses for, e.g., a brick or a newspaper; listing things that are impossible; giving unusual or original word or inkblot associations.

Judgment or Evaluative Abilities. Guilford applies the term 'evaluative' to judging the validity of logical trains of thought. But if there is a distinctive factor (or factors) it is probably involved more in reaching conclusions on the basis of 'practical feasibility, experience and social custom' rather than of logical necessity, as in the following item:

Ex. 65. Mrs. Williams picked up her raincoat, but after opening the front door to go, turned back and left the raincoat behind, because:
it was too heavy for her
she thought it would not rain
it would hide her new dress, if she wore it
her husband did not like her wearing a raincoat
her raincoat was rather too old to wear.

Thorndike suggested that 'social intelligence' could be distinguished from 'verbal' and 'practical intelligence'. Others have devised tests of critical or rational thinking, for example, judging whether a writer's arguments are logical or biased and emotional (cf. Watson and Glaser, 1942). As yet there is little evidence that such tests measure anything different from ordinary reading comprehension.

Finally, there are a number of tests in the fields of artistic, literary or musical evaluation, where the testee has to discriminate between examples of good and bad art, poetry, etc. Though such abilities probably depend largely on $g + v +$ attainment in these fields, they may well bring in additional factors of artistic taste (cf. Dewar, 1938).

SURVEY OF GROUP TESTS IN COMMON USE

A full list of tests published in Britain in 1956, with age ranges, times, publishers and prices is given elsewhere (Vernon, 1956). Buros's *Yearbooks* (1959) provide details and critical reviews of American and many English tests. Here we will merely draw attention to the main features of some of the most commonly used intelligence tests.

Oral Verbal Tests. There are two promising modern tests—Cornwell's *Group Test of Intelligence for Juniors* (1952) and Tomlinson's *Junior School Test* (1953); both have deviation I.Q. norms. They take several school periods to administer, and Tomlinson's, in particular, depends largely on the capacity to read words written on the blackboard. There is room for a shorter, simpler test which would be appropriate for first- and second-year juniors; for example, Ballard's *Group Test for Juniors* (1922) might be revised, shortened and renormed.

Oral Pictorial and Non-verbal. The Sleight *Non-Verbal Intelligence*

Test (1931) includes a good range of pictorial and figural items, and has been one of the most widely used junior school tests for many years. It provides M.A. norms only, whereas Mellone's *Moray House Picture Test* (1944) yields deviation I.Q.s. As already mentioned, tests of this type are unlikely to correlate anything like as highly with educational capacities as verbal tests; and they should not be thought of as giving a better measure of inborn ability, freed from environmental influence.

Wide-range Verbal Tests. Burt's *Northumberland Standardised Test No.* 3 (1925), Richardson's *Simplex Junior* (1932), and Schonell and Adams's *Essential Intelligence Tests* (1940) all embody a variety of the verbal item-types listed above. Their Mental Age norms run from 6 or 7 up to 16, but this means that their effective use is much more restricted, since they will not discriminate among dull children much below 9, nor bright ones above 12. Their Standard Deviations are fairly high, so that their I.Q.s are not comparable with WISC or Moray House I.Q.s; and, in these days of widespread coaching and familiarity with tests, their norms are some 5 to 10 points too generous. This is unfortunate, since they are among the most accessible and the easiest for teachers to apply in their own classes.

Verbal Tests for the Selection Examination. The tests issued annually for the 11-plus examination by Moray House and by the National Foundation for Educational Research are technically among the most sophisticated anywhere in the world. They provide highly reliable deviation I.Q.s over a narrow age-range (say, 10·0–12·0) which are comparable, to within 1 or 2 points, from year to year; (complete comparability for older versions is impossible because of the rather general upward trend since World War II; cf. Pilliner, 1960). The types of items are somewhat narrow because of the needs for easily intelligible instructions in omnibus tests and for easy scoring; also because the users—local education authorities—prefer a standard instrument. But more variety is apparent in recent years. A further interesting feature is that they do not claim to be 'intelligence tests'; the National Foundation has always referred to its series as Verbal Tests, and Moray House has now adopted the nomenclature Verbal Reasoning Tests. These tests are—wisely—not on general sale, though older versions may be released to research workers or other authorised persons.

Non-verbal Group Tests for Children and Adults. The Jenkins *Non-verbal Scale of Mental Ability* (1947), and a parallel form by Lee and Jenkins, provide reliable *g*-tests for 10- and 11-year olds with a minimum of verbal and spatial content. Their correlations with achievement in a grammar school are rather low, but they probably constitute better predictors of mathematical, scientific and technical aptitude than do verbal tests.

The National Foundation for Educational Research issues other non-verbal tests, together with a series containing mixed verbal and non-verbal sub-tests. Heim's Test *AH4*, for adolescents and normal adults, is also a combined test, probably having fairly strong number and spatial loadings, and is therefore useful for vocational purposes. Earle (1948) has published a series of *Duplex Tests* for 10-, 11-, 12- and 13-year olds respectively, containing a variety of verbal, numerical, spatial and mechanical items. Their aim is to show differential suitability for different types of secondary course—academic, technical, commercial, etc.—though they also yield a total result which can be converted to an I.Q.

The most widely used non-verbal test is Raven's *Progressive Matrices* (1938, 1947), of which there are several forms. Sets A, Ab and B are coloured, and are intended primarily for individual application to children of 5 years upwards or to senile patients. The 1938 series can be given in group form from 10 to adult levels, while the 1947 Sets I and II apply mainly to older children and superior adults. The tests are very easy to explain and administer and are usually given without time limit. Thus they are suitable for, say, mental hospital nurses to apply to defective or neurotic patients. The 1938 series was used (with a 20-minute time limit) with almost all naval and army recruits from 1941-4.

The National Institute of Industrial Psychology's *Group Test 70/23* (1939) may be recommended as a short but effective non-verbal test for 14 years up and adults. Finally, R. B. Cattell has published parallel forms of *Culture-free Intelligence Tests* (1949), Scale II for children and Scale III for adults. While we would reject the claim that any tests are culturally neutral, good evidence has been provided by Cattell that such tests give a fairer picture of intelligence level among linguistically handicapped persons such as foreign immigrants than do verbal tests.

Verbal Tests for Adolescents and Adults. Among the older tests, Cattell's (1935) *Intelligence Scales* II and III (Forms A and B) deserve mention as providing very thorough measures of $g + v$. Scale III is one of the most difficult available for superior adults. Though carefully standardised (Cattell, 1934), the tests seem to yield abnormally high I.Q.s, largely because they have big Standard Deviations.

Wiseman's *Manchester General Ability Test*, for 13–14½-year olds, and Thomson's *Moray House Adult Test*, for 13½-adult, follow the omnibus pattern of the 11-plus Moray House tests and provide deviation I.Q. norms.

The National Institute of Industrial Psychology's *Group Tests 33* (1923) and *Group Test 35* are suitable for grammar school and student populations, and have percentile norms. Like the Northumberland Test of Burt (who also devised Test 33), they are in battery form. *Group Test 90* (1948) is a similar test for the normal adult range, with norms for age groups from 21 to 60.

One other high-grade test, suitable only among the top 5 per cent of the population, is Heim's *AH5*, with verbal and non-verbal omnibus sections. Finally, there are a large number of tests devised by psychologists in the Armed Services and the Civil Service Commission for recruits, officers, clerks, administrators, etc., which are not, of course, publicly available. In general, they are chosen more for their relevance to a range of occupations than as tests of intelligence or other mental qualities or factors.

Chapter Six

EDUCATIONAL ATTAINMENT TESTS

IT is so convenient to be able to state that a pupil's reading is equal to that of the average 8-year old, or that he has an Arithmetic Quotient of 120, that we are apt to ignore the difficulties in educational measurement. What kind of reading or arithmetic has been tested? With many children there may be considerable unevenness in different aspects of a subject, and the test may or may not cover those aspects that the particular teacher, or modern educational opinion in general, regards as most important. The syllabus and the methods of teaching are likely to vary between, say, Scotland, Hampstead and Pembrokeshire so that it is unlikely that any one test is appropriate in all these areas. Alternatively, the child's teachers—knowing the content of the test— may have coached him and artificially raised his performance on those aspects without having improved his all-round attainment in the subject. Though it may sound heretical for a psychometrist to say so, the writer would hold that a child's score on a 10- to 40-minute test may often provide a less representative picture of his attainment than the impressions of the teacher who has observed the whole of his work over several months.

The apparent accuracy of educational age units, and of quotients derived therefrom, is also misleading. They assume that the average child gains an equivalent amount each year in each subject tested, though this obviously breaks down at the time of the 'push' for the 11-plus examinations and during the subsequent years in a secondary modern school. And they assume that standards remain constant, although some tests which are still in common use date back to 40 years, and there is clear proof of a widespread decline during World War II which has only partially been made up (cf. p. 163). Nor is it very meaningful to apply the same norms in a rural area, an industrial slum and a middle-class suburb. As suggested elsewhere, teachers and psychologists who use tests for educational guidance would do better to build up their own local percentile norms for the type of schools they are concerned with, and to revise these periodically, rather than rely on what are probably outdated national age norms (Vernon, 1956).

However, provided their limitations are borne in mind, attainment tests can admirably fulfil certain purposes. Group tests, such as those used at 11-plus, can give a fairly thorough, though not completely comprehensive, sampling of the skills which are regarded as important by most primary and secondary schools. Thus they are particularly useful for large-scale selection purposes, or for surveys of schools or areas, where it would be almost impossible to standardise the marking of more conventional, but subjective, examinations. Similar tests of more specific objectives are practically indispensable for investigations into teaching methods. For example, if an educationist wishes to study scientifically the advantages of television lessons, he should devise tests which will pinpoint the particular abilities that televised (and non-televised) instruction would be expected to develop. Many such tests are embodied in student research theses, but are unpublished. Note that for none of the purposes so far described does the problem of norms arise. In selection, Educational Quotients (corrected for age) are usually worked out by the same technique as that used for deviation I.Q.s (p. 50); but the crucial standard or borderline is generally set by the number of grammar-school places available. In surveys or experimental research, meaningful comparisons can be made between the scores of various groups without resort to age units or quotients.

However, let us first discuss tests used in educational guidance, whose aim is to assess the performance of individuals, or school classes, *with reference to some set of wider, external standards*, and thereby to judge whether children are failing to make reasonable educational progress, and if so what educational treatment is called for.

Individual Reading Tests. Though all aspects of reading overlap greatly, there is general agreement—backed up by factorial studies—that oral-pronouncing ability, reading speed and comprehension of sentences or paragraphs are relatively distinguishable. Word-pronouncing is generally tested by *Graded Vocabulary Tests*, containing lists of words ranging from those that can be read by 5- to 6-year olds up to those likely to be known only by 15-year olds or adults. Burt (1921), Vernon (1938) and Schonell (1945) have issued similar tests of this type. Vernon's test carries on up to higher age levels than the others, but its Reading Ages from 15 to 21 represent purely arbitrary units for expressing superior skill among older pupils or adults; and it is doubtful whether pronouncing ability is of much educational importance among older grammar-school pupils. Schonell's test, being the most recent, is likely to be the most suitable, in England at least. The norms for these tests differ, though not markedly, and a conversion table is available (Ministry of Education, 1950). The tests are easily administered and scored, in a few minutes per child, even by relatively inexperienced teachers; and they provide useful opportunities for noting types of error.

Ballard (1923) and Burt supply lists of monosyllables, from the number of which read aloud in one minute, reading speed can be gauged. But speed of reading continuous material is more important and this is included, along with measures of accuracy, in Burt's, Schonell's (1950) and Neale's (1958) prose-reading tests. In Burt's 'King of the Golden River' and Schonell's 'My Dog', time and errors are recorded, and thereafter a series of questions are asked to test understanding. Neither of these is likely to be sufficiently reliable to be worthwhile, and Watts's (1944) plan, in his *Holborn Reading Scale* for $6\frac{1}{2}$–$10\frac{1}{2}$ year children, of having a series of sentences graded in difficulty of pronunciation and of comprehension is superior. Unfortunately, Watts provides no comprehension norms; he seems to assume that children should be able to understand what they can pronounce. Much the best test of this type, over the junior school range, is Neale's *Analysis of Reading Ability*, which provides three parallel sets of passages, and up-to-date norms for the three aspects we have mentioned. Neale also allows for recording and tabulation of various types of error. Schonell has a series of supplementary (un-normed) diagnostic tests for very backward readers, designed to bring out their sources of difficulty; these include visual discrimination of words, knowledge of phonics, and tendency to reversals.

Daniels and Diack's (1958) *Standard Test of Reading Skill*, like the Holborn Scale, grades reading accuracy (though not comprehension) from 5 to 9 by means of sentences. It is supplemented by a large number of un-normed diagnostic tests, of visual and auditory discrimination, letter and word recognition, etc.

Vocabulary is usually tested as part of the Terman-Merrill or Wechsler intelligence scales. However, Raven's (1943) *Crichton* and *Mill Hill* vocabulary scales cover oral vocabulary from 4 years up to adult. In addition, there are multiple-choice versions, from 11 up, which can be given in written group form.

Spelling. While an individual reading or oral vocabulary test provides useful diagnostic information besides the quantitative score, there is little point in testing spelling or arithmetic individually. However, the following graded tests are more convenient for individual administration, since the child can be started at a level where he is likely to manage all the items (as in Binet-testing), and be stopped when he has reached his limit, whereas a much wider range of words would need to be given to cover the varied spelling abilities of a whole school class.

Burt's *Graded Vocabulary Test* provides 10 words for each year from 5 to 15. It is likely that both the norms, and the order of difficulty of the words, have altered since it was published in 1921. Schonell has two similar lists which are also quite old; standards may well have declined during World War II. Elsewhere (1932) he provides short graded tests of irregular and regular words, and supplementary individual diagnostic tests of visual and auditory recall (1942). Daniels and Diack's (1958) *Graded Spelling Test*, though consisting of 40 words only, probably gives adequate coverage of attainment in the junior school.

Arithmetic. The simplest tests for 6–8 year olds are Ballard's (1923) *One Minute Addition and Subtraction*, which consist of lists of combinations (2 plus 3, 6 plus 1 . . . 5 take away 2, etc.) to be done at speed. There are, however, no reliable norms except those published by Thomson and Lawley (1942) for 7-year olds. Burt's *Graded Oral Test*, containing 10 problems at each year from 5 to 15, is rather lengthy; but there is an abbreviated version with 4 problems a year (Burt, 1955a). Whether the order of difficulty and the norms still hold good is not known. Vernon's *Graded Arithmetic-Mathematics Test* (1949) is a written 20-minute group test, but it can generally be given individually in 10–15 minutes. There are 5 questions at each age level from 6 up to 21 (the units from 15 up being arbitrary). The upper-level items involve knowledge of secondary school mathematics:

Ex. 66. If log. 90 = 1·9542, what is log. 3?

GROUP TESTS

Many of the following are also often useful for guidance purposes.

Group Comprehension Tests. Once a child has crossed the initial hurdles in reading (usually at a Mental Age of about 8), and can recognise any new regular words for himself, his capacity to understand what he reads silently is what we chiefly wish to know. Reading comprehension tests at all levels from 7 or 8 to superior adult follow the same plan of presenting passages of prose; after reading each the testee has to answer one or two, or several, multiple-choice questions based on its content. These cover a variety of features—the extraction of specific information, determining the meaning of difficult words in their context, making inferences from the material or applying what has been read to fresh problems, evaluating the prejudices, mood or tone of the author, and so forth. Many investigations indicate that it is very difficult to disentangle such aspects of reading skill; whatever the 'faculty' or type of ability aimed at, they all measure much the same general capacity. Even Sentence Completion tests (similar to Ebbinghaus's test of intelligence, or Ex. 28) cover much the same ground as tests involving lengthy paragraphs, and mere size of vocabulary overlaps very highly despite its apparent 'lower order' of skill. Probably the subject-matter of the passage has more influence, at least in advanced tests; different testees vary according as it is literary, technical-scientific, philosophical, historical, etc.

In consequence, it is very difficult to construct reliable tests of this type without extensive trials of items, and they have to be quite lengthy to be of much use; (a typical American test for secondary pupils or students would contain perhaps 8 passages and 40 questions to be answered in 40 minutes). Thus there are few, if any, adequate examples in England. Lambert (1951) has published one for 7-year olds, lasting about 75 minutes. Highfield's *Kingston Test* (1954), with creative written responses, is suitable for 9-year olds. Schonell's (1950) *Silent Reading Tests A and B* are widely used, but are effective only over the $8\frac{1}{2}$- to 11-year range, and are too short for adequate reliability.

Most standardised tests of English for 11-plus selection contain reading comprehension sections, but also have other types of item (see below) to compensate for their weaknesses. There are no paragraph reading tests in this country for secondary pupils or students, though experimental ones have been constructed by Black (1954) and others. A sentence completion test by Watts and Vernon, covering reading ability from about 7-year to adult levels, has been widely used in Ministry of Education surveys of literacy (1950, 1957). This is not published; but Watts's similar *Sentence Reading Test* 1 (1958) and Daniels and Diack's *Graded Test of Reading Experience* (1958) are available for junior children; and another form by Vernon and Warden for 10-year to adult levels may be borrowed from the present writer by qualified persons. The following illustrates the kind of item:

Ex. 67. A highly cultured environment often boosts up the academic career of an otherwise (practical, absent, mediocre, brilliant, educated) student.

Spelling Tests. The dictated word test has the defect of depending greatly on the tester's clarity of enunciation and the pupils' familiarity with his pronunciation. This is partly, but not completely, overcome by saying each word in the context of a sentence:

Ex. 68. SEARCH—Search for the ball till you find it.

Lambert's (1951) *Seven-Plus Assessment* ensures that children know what words to write by means of pictures or stories; it takes approximately one hour.

American psychologists, however, prefer objective tests to dictation tests. These take various forms:

(*a*) Right-wrong—a series of words, those that are mis-spelt to be underlined.

(*b*) Multiple-choice.

Ex. 69. LOOK FOR   serch   scearch   sarch
                   sersh   search

(*c*) Skeleton word.

Ex. 70. LOOK FOR   s . . . ch

(*d*) One word in a sentence is mis-spelt; the testee finds and underlines, then rewrites it.

Ex. 71. Serch for the purse in the field. . . . . . .

Nisbet (1939) found that these all measure much the same ability as dictation tests, but Cook's (1932) more extensive series of comparisons indicated that the last type comes nearest to measuring the accuracy with which pupils will spell in their own compositions, i.e. in a situation where they do not know which words need special care. Though objective spelling items often occur in tests of English at 11-plus, and several other such tests are used by the Services, there are no published, standardised ones for British children.

Other English Skills. Schonell's *Diagnostic English Test* (1950) contains five sub-tests with separate age norms from 8 to 15.

I. Usage, including creative and choice-response items of the following types:

Ex. 72. We w . . . eating our dinner.

Ex. 73. Yesterday he $\frac{give}{gave}$ me a ball to play with.

II. Capitalisation and punctuation. Missing punctuation marks or wrong letters to be written in:

Ex. 74. joan asked are you going to scotland for your holidays

This is troublesome to score, and it is more usual to substitute multiple-choice form.

III. Vocabulary—multiple-choice.

IV. Sentence structure. Sets of two to four short sentences are given, to be re-ordered and combined into one complete sentence.

V. Composition (cf. below).

Burt's (1925) *Northumberland Standardised Test 2* is an older battery which likewise supplies separate norms for vocabulary, reading, spelling, also geography and history.

A number of unconventional tests of vocabulary, concept development and other aspects of language (rather than of school attainment) are given in Watts's *Language and Mental Development of Children* (1944).

English Tests in Selection at 11-plus. Moray House and National Foundation tests almost always take the omnibus form, with a hundred or more questions to be attempted in 40 or 45 minutes. They are standardised like intelligence tests to a mean quotient of 100 and Standard Deviation of 15 in each monthly age group. Reading comprehension, vocabulary and usage figure prominently, and sometimes spelling and punctuation. Other short blocks of items may include the following:

Finding Rhymes.

Ex. 75. PLOUGH rhymes with (cough, dough, cow, snuff, tough).

Explaining metaphors, e.g. playing with fire; choice-responses are given.
Choosing suitable titles for short poems.
Forming plurals, opposites, tenses, parts of speech, etc.

Ex. 76. AUDACITY. His behaviour was very . . . . . .

The National Foundation issues similar tests at a more advanced level, for 12- to 13-year pupils.

English tests of this kind are highly reliable, and easy to give and score, but they have aroused widespread criticism because—it is said—they require nothing but ticking and underlining, and therefore fail to measure a child's ability to express himself in writing. Though the argument is exaggerated—for at this level multiple-choice and creative tests measure very nearly the same thing—it is true that objective tests have had a bad effect on teaching in many junior schools. Children are trained at these items, since coaching probably pays considerable dividends, and get insufficient experience of free writing. The National Foundation for Educational Research, C. M. Fleming, and others have therefore devised tests which do involve creative responses but which are so formulated that there is very little room for subjectivity in scoring (cf. Vernon, 1957). The scoring is, of course, more onerous, but this seems worthwhile if the tests have better pedagogical effects. Some examples follow.

Sentence completion with single words.

Ex. 77. A tricycle has three . . . . . .

Writing a grammatical ending to a sentence.

Ex. 78. I told him that he ought to . . . .

Writing a suitable beginning to a sentence.

Ex. 79. . . . . as it was beginning to rain.

Rephrasing sentences.

Ex. 80. Jim stole the jam from the larder.
        The jam . . . .

Reported speech.

Ex. 81. "May I go home now?" said Mary.

Mary asked . . . . home now.

Writing a complete sentence in answer to a question.

Ex. 82. Why are you late for school, John? . . . .

Tests used for selection at 11-plus are not published, for obvious reasons; but the National Foundation has issued five *English
Progress Tests* (for 8+, 10+, 11+, 12+, 13+), wholly or mainly
composed of such items.

It should be noted that both these and the fully objective group
tests give a much broader sampling of English abilities, are more
reliable and better standardised, than most of the tests with age
norms that are commonly used in educational guidance. But
clearly they provide less information regarding the particular
aspects of English in which the pupil is backward or advanced.

Handwriting and Composition. Burt (1921) provides norms for
speed of writing simple sentences, but these are probably out of
date. For it has been shown that Scottish pupils, at least, aged
11-12, write at only one-third the speed of their American counter-
parts (Smith, 1951). The quality of handwriting or of composition
cannot, of course, be measured objectively. But the quality or
product scale technique is of considerable help. Typical specimens
are reproduced, say one for each age group. A child then writes
the same passage or a composition on the same topic as in the
standard specimen, and his product is compared with the specimens until one is found which it most closely resembles in all-
round quality.

Burt's quality of handwriting scale is still the best available,
though it is no longer of much use at the upper end, since quality
and legibility tend to decline rather than improve after 11 years.
Moreover, a greater diversity of styles is favoured nowadays in
different junior schools. Burt also gives specimen compositions,
from $7\frac{1}{2}$ to $14\frac{1}{2}$, on the topic 'School', while Schonell has provided alternative scales on a variety of topics (1942, 1950).

Arithmetic. Burt's *Written Graded Mechanical Arithmetic* (Test IX),
Four Rules (Tests XI–XIV) and *Written Graded Problems* (Test X),
also Highfield's *Southend Test* and Schonell's (1950) *Essential
Mechanical* and *Problem Arithmetic Tests* (two forms) all provide

age norms from about 7 to 14 or 15. It is not known whether these norms still hold after the decline during World War II. The National Foundation issues several well-standardised Mechanical Arithmetic tests for 8–9 year olds.

Most group tests, either for selection at 11-plus or for wider age ranges, contain two sections, each of 20 to 25 minutes, one covering mechanical, the other problem, arithmetic. Examples include Lambert's *Seven Plus Assessment* (with 20 minutes for each of the Four Rules), Fleming's *Cotswold* and *Kelvin* tests, the National Foundation's *Arithmetic Progress Test C*, and the annual Moray House or National Foundation arithmetic tests. More advanced is the National Foundation's *Mathematics Test I*.

These tests, too, are often criticised in that they stress working at speed, and give insufficient scope for ingenuity and application to long problems. But any assessment of such qualities would be likely to bring in subjective judgment. For the diagnosis of backwardness and for guidance purposes, tests which break down arithmetic into separate topics are more useful (cf. Schonell, 1957). Burt's *Northumberland Standardised Test No. 1* (1925) has seven sections, and could be very useful if the norms were brought up to date. Schonell's *Diagnostic Arithmetic Tests* (1950) cover all the fundamental combinations, graded sums in the Four Rules, and mental arithmetic. For maximum information they should be given untimed, spread over several periods. However, they can be applied with time limits totalling some 80 minutes, and norms are provided for each sub-test from 7 to 15 years.

For a relatively quick survey of attainment either in junior or in secondary schools, Vernon's *Arithmetic-Mathematics Test* (already described) can be given in group form with a 20-minute limit. The only detailed test of grammar school mathematics published in this country is Walton's *Geometry Attainment Test* (1948) for pupils aged 12–16+.

Other School Subjects. Apart from experimental tests used, for example, in research investigations, but not standardised or published, there are scarcely any tests in languages, social studies, science or other subjects. Tests of French vocabulary and grammar, by Percival(1951), are available for 1st to 5th year grammar pupils; and Cohen's (1949) somewhat more extensive French tests, standardised on 1st to 3rd year Australian pupils, are sometimes used. But we must admit a marked contrast with America, where numerous tests in every school subject are available for any level up to 4th year university. The difference arises partly because secondary school and university syllabuses are so varied that there is little common ground on which to base tests. But also, of course, our secondary grammar schools are geared to training pupils for conventional examinations, and see little point in assessing their attainment along various lines with objective tests which, by their very nature, cannot measure quite the same abilities as do G.C.E. or university scholarship examinations.

Chapter Seven

THE INTERPRETATION OF INTELLIGENCE AND EDUCATIONAL TEST RESULTS

INEVITABLY this chapter is rather more technical than the rest. But no one should be encouraged to apply tests, to make use of their results or to criticise them, unless he is willing to acquaint himself with certain basic psychometric principles.

UNITS OF MENTAL GROWTH

The first problem to be faced has already been touched on briefly, namely the irregularities in Mental and Educational Age units (p. 92). In measuring lengths with a ruler, the distance from 12 to 13 inches is the same as that from 2 to 3 inches. But it is most unlikely that mental growth from 12 to 13 years is the same as that from 2 to 3. The traditional method of scoring intelligence tests in Mental Age units and calculating Intelligence Quotients, however, makes just this assumption. If a person of average intelligence is to obtain an I.Q. of 100 at every age, the graph of mental growth must take the form shown in Fig. 4*a*. But no psychologist believes that growth in ability is linear throughout childhood, or that it stops abruptly at 15 or any other age. There is no really watertight method of determining the true course of development, and the attempts made by Thurstone, Dearborn, Heinis and others are somewhat discrepant. But Fig. 4*b* is certainly a nearer approximation. The first few years are particularly uncertain, but from 5 to 10 there is a period when growth can reasonably be regarded as roughly linear; then a slowing down and later a decline. No one individual, of course, conforms closely to this average. The slope is steeper for bright and gentler for dull children; in addition, each child is likely to show irregularities, spurts and plateaus, depending on intellectual stimulation and experience at home and at school, and on emotional security or instability.

We have seen also that intelligence is not a single, unitary entity; it comprises a host of overlapping functions which doubtless develop at different rates at different times. Hence any curve of

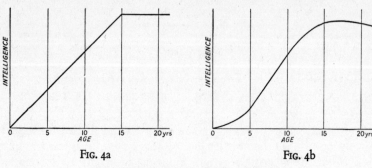

FIG. 4a   FIG. 4b

THE GROWTH OF INTELLIGENCE

mental development will vary more or less with the tests used. The age at which growth ceases likewise varies with the test, the individual and his environment. It is sometimes stated that duller children reach their maximum at an earlier age than bright ones, but the evidence for this is dubious. More probably, as will be shown in Chapter Nine, this age depends on the length and quality of schooling received by the adolescent, or the intellectually stimulating or inhibiting nature of his job and leisure pursuits.

Educational Age units likewise vary in size. Among British pupils the largest increment tends to occur in the final year of the junior school, and after this there is little further improvement in the average secondary modern pupil. But this varies, of course, in different schools and in different subjects. Mechanical arithmetic, for example, tends to drop back from 12 to 14, whereas reading comprehension and technical abilities are more likely to improve and to go on doing so after leaving school.

Our knowledge of such growths and declines is admittedly rudimentary. But enough has been said to show that the linear development of Fig. 4a gives a very poor approximation except over the limited 5 to 10 age-range. Hence I.Q.s and E.Q.s calculated from age scores by formulae which assume such linearity will inevitably show fluctuations or irregularities, particularly when the scores reach 11 and over. The Terman-Merrill scale makes some attempt to allow for the gradual tailing off between 12 and 16 in its I.Q. Tables, but this device, too, is an oversimplification. The only satisfactory and rational solution is to abandon the age unit and quotient system of measuring abilities, and to substitute percentile or standard score norms for each separate age-group. Unfortunately, the age system has become too widely known to, and accepted by, school teachers, medical officers and others concerned with children's development to be discarded easily, and it is undeniably convenient over the primary school range. But even if we have to continue to use it for many years to come, we should be aware of its defects.

THE NORMAL DISTRIBUTION OF ABILITIES

We must consider next the implications of a very fundamental principle in mental testing—the tendency for human abilities to be normally distributed. If a large, unselected group of children or adults is tested, and the numbers obtaining each score, or I.Q. or E.Q. are plotted, the graph usually approximates to the symmetrical, bell-shaped curve known as the *normal* or *Gaussian distribution*. The largest proportion score near to the average or *mean*, and there are fewer and fewer as we proceed to either extreme. In practice, the graph is always somewhat irregular unless the numbers are very large; and if the group has been creamed, or in other ways selected, it will, of course, tend to become skewed rather than symmetrical.[1] But in any large, unselected group, divergence from normality arises chiefly because the units of measurement are unequal. Suppose, for example, a test contained a lot of easy and medium items, but only a few, steeply graded difficult ones, then an otherwise normal distribution might assume the shape shown in Fig. 5. But if, now, the higher units (at the right-hand end) expanded in width and correspondingly decreased in height, the graph would become symmetrical again.

Different tests of intelligence generally yield normal distributions of I.Q.s, but their curves often differ in spread or range. Psychometrists measure this spread by the *Standard Deviation* (S.D.) or sigma (σ), which is roughly equal to one-sixth of the total range.[2] Thus the Stanford-Binet scale generally gave an I.Q. distribution with a S.D. of 15. All except a very small proportion of its I.Q.s fell between 145 and 55 (i.e. $100 + 3\sigma$ and $100 - 3\sigma$). All but the highest and lowest $2\frac{1}{4}$ per cent fell between 130 and 70

[1] For a fuller description, see Vernon (1956).
[2] It is calculated by squaring the amount by which each score differs from the mean, averaging these squares and taking the square root.

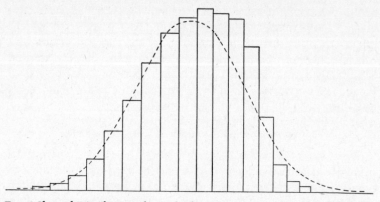

FIG. 5 Skewed Distribution obtained when upper items are too steeply graded in difficulty. (Dotted Line represents Normal Distribution, with Evenly Graded Items.

(i.e. 100 $\pm$ 2σ); about two-thirds between 115 and 85 (100 $\pm$ 1σ), and about one-half between 110 and 90 (100 $\pm$ $\frac{2}{3}\sigma$). Many of the older group tests, however, yielded much larger S.D.s, 20 or even 25 to 30. This meant that fewer testees obtained I.Q.s close to 100, and more got very high *or* low ones. Thus, if the same group of children took the Stanford-Binet and a Cattell group test, the mean I.Q. on both tests might be 100, but some of the Cattell I.Q.s might range all the way from about 30 to 170. The Terman-Merrill scale is particularly confusing (cf. p. 55); for while the S.D. averages 16$\frac{1}{2}$, it goes as low as 12 at 6 years, and rises to a maximum of 20 at 11 years. This means that an I.Q. of 130 represents very high intelligence (99th percentile) in a 6-year old, but only moderately high (93rd percentile) in a 12-year old.

Similar differences occur between educational tests. For example, Reading Quotients from a Graded Word test tend to show a narrower spread than those from Schonell's Silent Reading tests. Children who are 2 years backward in the former may score 3 years backward on the latter. Yet this is purely a matter of units; it does not signify that they are 'worse' at comprehension than at oral reading. Ordinary school examinations likewise tend to give normal or slightly skewed distributions of marks, which often differ considerably in spread as between different markers or different subjects. For instance, the range of percentage marks in arithmetic is almost always much wider than that in English examinations. As pointed out elsewhere (Vernon, 1956), such marks cannot properly be compared or combined unless the S.D.s are adjusted.

The origin of such differences is somewhat obscure, though it is certain that one major factor is the degree of heterogeneity of the items composing the test. In a group test like Cattell's almost all the items are very similar in type, whereas in the Stanford-Binet they were quite diverse. In addition, certain abilities seem to have an intrinsically smaller spread than others. More concrete ones, such as counting pennies and copying a square or diamond, spread out the testees less than do reasoning and orientation items, which involve the mental organisation of abstractions.[1]

Among tests scored by age units such differences in spread are unavoidable, and there are no grounds for deciding that any one S.D. of I.Q.s is the 'right' or 'true' one. Thus the important practical conclusion follows that the tester should never quote an I.Q. or E.Q. without mentioning the test used, since the same quotient from different tests often represents different levels of ability. To make these comparable they can be adjusted so that their S.D.s are equated. For example, Cattell I.Q.s can be made approximately equivalent to Binet ones by multiplying any deviation from 100 by $\frac{15}{25}$. Thus Cattell 150 = Binet 130, and Cattell 75 = Binet 85. Although Stanford-Binet is no longer used, it provides a useful standard because we became accustomed, during 1916 to 1937, to regarding I.Q. 70 as the rough borderline of mental deficiency, below which fell some $2\frac{1}{2}$ per cent of the population. Similarly, a reading or arithmetic quotient of 85, that is 1 S.D. below the mean, has become widely accepted as a borderline of educational backwardness, which cuts off the bottom 15 to 16 per cent of the primary school population. Burt provided a useful definition of backwardness which fits in with this: the backward child is one who, in the middle of his school career, at 10·0 years, cannot manage the work of the class a year younger. Since this younger class would range in age from 8·5 to 9·5, our backward 10-year old would fall below average 8·5-year olds, and so would obtain a quotient below 85. But we must emphasise that the S.D. of 15 is a convention, and that the quotients from most age-scored tests yield higher figures.

[1] Cf. Sare (1951). Other influences, probably of lesser importance, are discussed by Cattell and Vernon (1937).

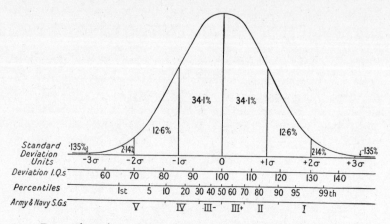

FIG. 6 The Relation between the Normal Distribution, Deviation
I.Q.s and Percentiles.

DEVIATION QUOTIENTS OR STANDARD SCORES

We are now in a position to understand why Moray House and most other modern tests are standardised as described in Chapter Three. Much as the parabola or hyperbola have their characteristic algebraic equations, so has the normal curve. In any normal distribution, $2\frac{1}{2}$ per cent of testees score 2σ or more above the mean, and $2\frac{1}{2}$ per cent are 2σ or more below. So if we choose a mean of 100 and a S.D. of 15, the $97\frac{1}{2}$th percentile corresponds to a standard score of 130 and the $2\frac{1}{2}$th percentile to 70. Unlike the classical quotients, these scores are comparable from any one test, or from one age group, to another. Fig. 6 illustrates such a distribution, and shows the proportions of cases falling within 1σ, 2σ, etc., on either side of the mean. The corresponding deviation I.Q.s and percentiles are given below.[1]

This method has the additional advantage of compensating for irregularities in the size of the original or raw-score units. Given a distribution like that shown in Fig. 5, the conversion of percentiles to standard scores would automatically have the effect of expanding the over-large units at the top end.

Standard scores, then, do constitute an equal-interval scale.

[1] Readers who wish to obtain more accurate conversions of percentiles to standard deviation units, or vice versa, are advised to use the graph facing p. 50 of *The Measurement of Abilities* (Vernon, 1956).

The same is not true of percentiles. These are always rectangularly, not normally, distributed. For by definition, one-tenth of all testees obtain percentiles between the 100th and 90th, one-tenth between the 90th and 80th, and so on. Hence percentile units are very unequal at different parts of the scale. The difference between the 95th and 85th or between the 5th and 15th percentiles is more than twice as big as the difference between the 45th and 55th. (That is why Army S.G. units are chosen to cut off 10:20: 40:20:10 per cent respectively. These percentages correspond, rather inaccurately, to equal units along a normal curve.) So although percentile norms for tests are rather easily obtained and simply interpreted, they are apt to be misleading. For instance, one should never add together nor average percentile scores.

CRITICISM OF THE ASSUMPTION OF NORMAL DISTRIBUTION

In the previous section we have admitted that a normal distribution is often imposed on a set of test scores. This had led some critics to dispute the whole conception of abilities being normally distributed.[1] Probably these critics are objecting chiefly to the notion that intellectual differences are innate or genetically determined. But the normal distribution is not dependent on the conception of heredity. Whether a man's intelligence level results from the operation of numerous genes or whether, as others believe, it results from the effects of factors in his upbringing, it would still be reasonable to expect to find the majority of intelligences near the mean and relatively few very high or very low ones. We would agree that the range of this distribution may well be magnified through the influence of socio-economic and educational differences, but not that the tendency to normal shape is an artefact. The evidence for this view is as follows:

(i) If we take any bodily skill which *can* be measured in objective physical units, such as tapping speed, the distribution is

[1] Cf. Simon (1953). One must admit, too, that test-constructors are apt to argue in a circle, in that they claim to find normal distributions from tests into which normality has been introduced, as it were, by the back door. If they try out a large batch of items, and select equal numbers of items at each level of difficulty (say, 85 per cent + pass-rate, 75–84 per cent, 65–74 per cent . . . 14 per cent and under), then the total scores on the selected items will inevitably tend to be normal.

always normal or only slightly skewed. Proceeding to tests that involve a stronger admixture of intellectual factors, there are no signs of departure from this same shape. Thus there is no reason to suppose that purely mental tests, which are scored in psychological units, would differ either.

(ii) The original Binet-Simon scale was constructed entirely without reference to statistical distributions. Yet, over a limited age-range at least, the I.Q.s it yielded conformed closely to normality. Probably there were divergences in the youngest and in the oldest age-groups because the scale failed to cover the lowest and highest levels adequately, and because of the (already admitted) irregularities of M.A. units above about 11 years.

Stanford-Binet and Terman-Merrill I.Q. distributions do sometimes depart appreciably from normality (McMeeken, 1939; Scottish Council, 1949), but this occurs chiefly at the level where irregularity of M.A. units is most likely to arise. In any case, the distribution at any one age is so dependent on the difficulties of the particular items falling round about that level that the observed irregularities neither prove, nor disprove, the hypothesis of normality. In addition, there seems to be a 'bump' at the bottom end of the curve, representing the imbeciles and idiots with I.Q.s below 40 who are the result of pathological causes or rare genes rather than of the usual genetic plus environmental causes (cf. p. 141).

(iii) Similar discrepancies do occur with group tests which, as Keats (1950) has shown, sometimes give raw score distributions conforming more closely to what is known as the Beta Function form than to normality. It seems doubtful, however, whether such tests possess sufficient headroom or sufficient footroom, i.e. enough difficult or easy items respectively, to spread out the testees. A crucial confirmatory experiment was carried out by Burt (1957): a series of test items which fell at equal steps of difficulty and which covered the whole range was selected by psychophysical techniques without reference to the normal curve. The scores of an unselected group on this scale gave an approximately normal distribution.

In conclusion, it is—as the critics claim—practically impossible to prove that mental abilities are normally distributed. But there is no logical reason, nor any strong evidence, for suggesting any other type of distribution. Psychologists have therefore come to accept this dogma, since it provides such a convenient basis for test construction and for statistical analysis of test scores. And they infer that mental tests which do yield such distributions are scored in equal units, whereas the units of tests that fail to show normality (as in Fig. 15) are unequal.

A qualification should be made regarding special abilities and attainments, as distinct from intelligence. It may well be that the upper reaches of achievement in special fields bring in a different principle. Burt (1943) suggests that measures of *productivity* are likely to be strongly positively skewed, i.e. that a very few individuals may show really outstanding achievement. This is obviously true of income, and it seems to apply to artistic, literary and scientific output. The musical genius falls far beyond the normal distribution of musical ability that applies to the majority of the population. Possibly the same phenomenon occurs with the talents of school pupils, though it is difficult to say how far superior is the exceptional musician, actor, artist or model-maker to the average until we can devise equal-unit measuring scales.

One other point to note is that tests are occasionally constructed with the intention of yielding non-normal distributions. If they are to be used for selecting, say, the best 20 per cent of a group, then they are more efficient if as many items as possible are chosen at an appropriately difficult borderline.[1] The distribution is then highly skewed and gives excellent discrimination at the 80th percentile, but does not bother about accurate discrimination between average and poor testees.

THE RELIABILITY OF INTELLIGENCE AND OTHER TESTS

When a child is retested or given a parallel form of a test, his second I.Q. may differ to some extent from his first one for any of a number of reasons. So far we have discussed only the first two in the following list, and have seen that these can be controlled or eliminated by substituting percentiles or standard scores for age units and quotients.

1. Irregularities in scoring units, particularly over 10 to 15 years.
2. Differences in spread between different tests.

[1] Lord (1955) shows that the optimum pass-rate, for this purpose, should be around 35 per cent rather than 20 per cent.

3. Chance differences: (*a*) inadequate sampling; (*b*) disturbances at the time of one or both tests; (*c*) differences in health, mood, motivation, etc.

4. Inaccuracies in norms.

5. Differences in the factor content, i.e. the kind of intelligence the tests measure.

6. Regression effects.

7. Changes due to practice or coaching.

8. Environmental influences and personality changes producing genuine rises or declines between one testing and another.

3. *Chance Factors.* Psychometrists draw a broad distinction between influences that tend to operate at random, affecting some testees one way, some another, and systematic influences that are apt to affect all members of a group, even if to varying extents. The two types often overlap—for example, motivational influences may operate systematically. But the distinction is useful because, as we shall see, the effects of the former conform to a certain statistical pattern.

Each item of a test is a sample of the ability we are trying to measure, and if there are too few samples or weak ones, the results are naturally unreliable. Some group tests cover the lower ranges of ability adequately but tail off at the top end. For example, if the test norms run like this:

Score	8	20	30	39	46	50	53
M.A.	7	8	9	10	11	12	13

it is very unlikely that the test can discriminate reliably around the 12-year mental level.

There are a host of other chance factors that may upset particular children's performance—the teacher looking over their shoulders, a singing lesson next door, inattention when the instructions are being explained, misleading 'sets' such as applying methods which worked in a previous test to the present one, copying from neighbours, putting right answers in the wrong spaces on the test blank, turning over two pages at once; also mistakes made by the scorer in marking or in adding up right answers. One reason for the superiority of individual tests is, as we have seen, that the tester can control many of these extraneous influences.

Testees vary too in their state of health, freshness or fatigue, and in keenness or co-operativeness, anxiety or undue excitability. While the tester should do his best to control these and to induce an attitude of confidence, concentration and carefulness, their effects should not be exaggerated (cf. p. 74). At the same time we have admitted that very young, or maladjusted, children must be handled individually.

Now if the differences between scores at a first and second test, which have arisen from such non-systematic factors, are tabulated, it is found that they too tend to fall into a normal distribution. A majority of children score round about the same, or rise or fall slightly, but a few show much larger discrepancies. This is the statistical pattern already referred to. Moreover, we can determine the spread of this distribution—now called the Standard Error or S.E. rather than the S.D.—provided we know the correlation coefficient between the two testings, and thus can predict how frequently large discrepancies are likely to occur.[1] With a correlation, or reliability coefficient of 0·91 (for a test with S.D. of I.Q. 15), the S.E. is $4\frac{1}{2}$ points. This means that two-thirds of the discrepancies or errors will lie between $+4\frac{1}{2}$ and $-4\frac{1}{2}$ I.Q. points; and the median or typical child's error will be only 3 points either way.[2] But as the total range of any normal distribution is about 6 times its S.D., there will be occasional discrepancies of 14 points or over either way. These are likely to occur only about once in a thousand cases. Similarly, discrepancies of $2 \times$ S.E. or ± 9 points or more occur in nearly 5 per cent.

Note that, while the Standard Error provides us with a most useful index of the liability of the I.Q. (or other score) to error, it cannot possibly tell us *which* children's scores are erroneous to a small or large extent, nor whether any particular child is too high or too low. It is only an overall statistical quantity. Another important point is that the reliability coefficient itself has little meaning in the absence of information regarding the group from

[1] More accurately, the S.E. defines the extent of discrepancies between obtained scores and hypothetical 'true' scores that the testees would obtain if the test were perfectly reliable. The discrepancies between any pair of tests (with a coefficient of 0·91) will be nearly half as large again as those quoted; and if children are frequently retested, their greatest discrepancies will be twice as large, ranging up to about ± 27 points.

[2] This figure, namely about two-thirds of the S.E., is referred to as the Probable Error or P.E.

whose scores it was calculated. If the group was very heterogeneous, comprising children of a wide age-range, it will be
boosted; but if the group was unusually homogeneous, say 12-
year-olds in a grammar school, it will be far lower. The usual
practice is to calculate reliability coefficients in a single primary
grade or in a complete age-group. Fortunately the S.E. is not
affected in this way by heterogeneity.

In a single age-group, a reliability coefficient of 0·91 is regarded as reasonably high. Occasionally coefficients as large as
0·96 are claimed. The S.E. then drops to 3 points. Even here errors
of up to ±10 points are possible, though very rare. On the other
hand, reliabilities are often lower, especially over longer periods,
when some of the other influences listed above (factor content,
environmental effects, etc.) alter markedly. On retesting after 2
to 5 years or so the reliability coefficient may drop to as low as 0·6,
and the S.E. rise to $9\frac{1}{2}$ points. The typical child still alters only by
±6 or 7 points, and half the children by this amount or less. But
the other half show discrepancies up to 25 or 30 points.[1] Results
obtained from pre-school tests are extremely unreliable (cf. p. 64).
It is commonly found also that scores are more unstable among
above average than among duller children, as in the Terman-
Merrill test (p. 56).

This considerable degree of variability is not usually realised by
test users who lack statistical training, though it has always been
stressed by psychologists from Burt and Terman onwards. It
implies that one should never think of a child's I.Q. (or other test
result) as accurate to 1 per cent. Rather an I.Q. of, say, 95 should
be thought of as a kind of region or general level. For a few weeks
or months to come there are even chances that it falls between 92
and 98; and the odds are about 10 to 1 that his I.Q. lies within
the range 88 to 102. But the possibilities of much larger discrepancies should not be forgotten. Over several years, say from 5
to 10 or from 11 to 15, the most we can say is that there is fair
certainty (i.e. 10 to 1) of its lying between 80 and 110.

However, this changeability should not be exaggerated. If we
studied school examinations in the same way, we should certainly

[1] Here also the figures refer to discrepancies from hypothetical true scores.
Between the first test and the second the median variation will be ±8, the
maximum about ±36; and with numerous tests over 5 years, the median child
will vary ±13 points, the most irregular up to 50 or even 60 points.

find them at least as variable, probably more so because of the subjective element in marking. Apart from a few exceptional cases, children do stay within the same intelligence band or region, at least from 5 on; they do not normally shift from below average to superior or vice versa. Moreover, as shown below, it is still possible to make valuable predictions of educational and vocational success several years ahead on the basis of tests. Note also that two tests are more reliable than one, and a series of tests at intervals better still. There is much to be said for applying an individual test to each child shortly after entering the infant school, then a group oral or a non-verbal test at 7 years, and group verbal tests at 2-yearly intervals thereafter, and putting the results on a cumulative record card. Many children will show a fairly steady level throughout; some may present a rather consistent rising or falling trend; the majority will be rather jerky, but wild fluctuations will be comparatively rare.

4. *Inaccuracies in Test Norms.* The results on one test are sometimes higher all round than on another because the norms of the one are too lenient or of the other too severe. Differences of 5 I.Q. points or more are not uncommon, though the very thoroughly standardised Moray House tests seldom vary more than 1 point. Test constructors should not be blamed too harshly for this state of affairs. The difficulties of getting really representative cross-sections of the population are seldom realised.[1] Any one school usually draws mainly from a certain socio-economic stratum; hence the average I.Q. in a good suburban neighbourhood may well be 15 points higher than in a poor slum or a remote rural area. Picking a few good, mediocre and poor schools on the basis of personal hunch or convenience is unlikely to yield an accurate representation. The theoretical principles of systematic sampling are well-established (cf. McNemar, 1940a), but it is not easy, particularly for the private investigator, to apply them in practice. At the secondary school selection stage, tests are often standard-

[1] Our recommendation for substituting deviation quotients at each age level for age units and quotients complicates matters still further. For it means that samples at every age should be representative in spread as well as in mean score. Thus, strictly, we should not miss out the mental defectives at the bottom end or the private and public school pupils at the top end. Perhaps it will be simpler tacitly to omit these, taking 15 as the agreed S.D. in maintained schools and admitting that the figure should be somewhat higher in really complete age-groups.

ised on the whole age-group within an area that is being examined. Even then it does not follow that the same norms are applicable to other areas (cf. p. 173).

It is still more difficult to get representative samples of 0- to 5-year olds or of persons aged over 15, and most constructors of tests for adolescents and adults content themselves with percentile norms for limited groups. Nevertheless, Cattell (1934) and Raven (1939) have built up good cross-sections of the population on the basis of occupations (adults), or fathers' occupations (children).

Educational tests are if anything more tricky because standards are more likely to alter with time. It would appear that national performance in most subjects tended to rise between the wars, so that by 1939 the norms for many of Burt's tests, published in 1921, were too lenient. Then during World War II there was a serious loss of 1 to 2 years of Educational Age, probably differing according to the impact of war conditions in different parts of the country. Changing conceptions of the importance of formal subjects may also have affected standards. They seem to be rising again now, but the overall picture can only be described as chaotic. Surveys of school populations using tests from the 1930s are showing 30 per cent or so of children to be seriously backward, those using post-war tests only 15-20 per cent; with Burt's tests the figures are likely to be intermediate. In individual educational guidance, too, a child's Educational Age will vary appreciably with the particular tests and standardisations employed. No doubt this will be sorted out eventually, but the amount of work involved in accurate standardisation precludes any easy solution. The experienced educational psychologist may be able to trace his path clearly in this tangle; but other test users would be better advised to confine themselves to recently standardised tests, or to build up percentile norms for older tests in their own schools or districts.

5. *Changes in Test Content*. Different results from different tests often arise, not because the tests are untrustworthy in themselves but because they differ in content. We should never expect to get identical I.Q.s from a group verbal intelligence test and a set of performance tests, nor identical Reading Quotients from Graded Word and Paragraph Comprehension tests. To a lesser extent, there will be differences between group verbal tests consisting of different types of item, or given under different conditions of

timing. We have already drawn attention to the variations in factor content of the Terman-Merrill scale at different ages (p. 55). Probably the main reason why pre-school and infant tests show so little correlation with later intelligence is because the former rely mainly on perceptual and motor performances. Not until children begin to express their ability largely through language, after about 5 years, can reasonable stability be expected. We are far too readily influenced by mere names: and just because tests for 3-year, 6-year, 10-year children and adults are labelled intelligence tests, we expect them all to measure the same thing.

6. *Regression Effects*. If we select a group of tall parents, averaging say 10 inches above the mean for the population, and measure the heights of their offspring when they grow up, the average of the latter will be found to be only about 5 inches above the mean. Conversely, if we take very short parents, their children will also tend to be of below average height, but not so much so as their parents. Psychometrists call this regression to the mean. It is not difficult to see why this must occur. There is a correlation of only 0·5 between the heights of parents and offspring, and this means that many of the tallest parents have relatively short offspring, and some of the tallest offspring are born to moderately tall parents. Thus it is equally true that if we select tall (or short) offspring, the mean heights of their parents likewise regress to nearer the mean.

Similarly, then, when we select a group of superior children on the basis of one test, we must expect to find their average score somewhat lower on a second test; conversely, a group of dull or backward ones will always show an apparent rise. But this follows simply from the fact that the two tests do not correlate perfectly, and it may have no special psychological significance.[1] It does not represent some kind of compensatory weakness among bright children, nor strength among dull children—any more than regression of heights represents a compensatory characteristic of tall or short parents and offspring. Yet time and again this error crops up in interpreting test results. Here are some examples.

---

[1] The amount of regression depends directly on the lowness of correlation. If the mean score of the selected group is x above the mean of the total group, then the mean at the second test will be rx (provided the S.D. remains the same). Hence, with $r = 0·5$, the average deviation of parents from the mean is halved in their offspring. And in Example (i) below, if $r = 0·75$, the mean I.Q. of 120 drops to 115.

(i) Pupils selected for grammar school usually have I.Q.s 110 upwards, and average about 120: retested a year or two later the average has apparently fallen to 115.

(ii) Children certified as educationally subnormal, largely on the basis of verbal (Terman-Merrill) test, have I.Q.s around 70. Since the correlation of verbal with performance tests is only about 0·6, their mean performance test I.Q. must be about 80. But there is nothing startling about their practical ability being, on average, superior to their verbal ability. It happens because some of the lowest scorers on performance tests did not fall in the original E.S.N. group.

(iii) Children who are backward in ordinary school work apparently make larger gains when taught by films (or any other novel teaching device) than those who are advanced. The reason is merely that the correlation between ordinary school work and the test applied after film (or other) instruction is less than 1·0.

(iv) A group of backward readers is sent to a clinic or a special class, and after a term or so shows some improvement which is attributed to the special coaching. But as the correlation between the initial reading test and the final one is certain to be less than 1·0, a good deal of this improvement may be spurious. Only if the regression effect is allowed for, or if the remedial coaching group is compared with another equally backward group of pupils who are not coached, is this inference justified (cf. Curr and Gourlay, 1953).

7 and 8. Adequate discussion of practice and environmental effects requires separate chapters. The main point to notice here is that the very large numbers of other influences mentioned so far must be allowed for before we are entitled to suspect the existence of genuine environmental alterations. For instance, when an 11-year old gets 130 I.Q. on his selection test, and 110 if retested with Terman-Merrill or some different group test, it is very tempting to infer that he has been coached on the first test or that his ability has declined. It is as likely, or more so, that differences in norms, in units of measurement, in S.D., or in factor content, or chance influences (unreliability) are responsible.

COMPARING DIFFERENT ABILITIES

So far we have been concerned mainly with hazards in the interpretation of scores on a single test or parallel tests. Unreliability is going to arise, too, in comparing different tests, as when we contrast Educational with Intelligence Quotients, or verbal with performance test results. Inaccuracies in the norms of either test, differences in spread, or different degrees of practice can obviously stultify one's conclusions. But apart from these, the reliability of a difference between two tests depends not only on the reliabilities of the separate tests, but also on the smallness of correlation between them. If, as often happens, they overlap rather highly, the unreliability of any differences is enhanced; in other words, only the biggest score differences have any significance at all. Table IV illustrates the reliability of score differences at certain levels of test reliability (r_{AA} and r_{BB}) and inter-correlation (r_{AB}).[1]

TABLE IV

RELIABILITY COEFFICIENTS OF DIFFERENCE SCORES

r_{AB}	·1	·3	·5	·7
·9	·89	·86	·80	·67
r_{AA} ·8	·78	·72	·60	·33
and ·7	·67	·57	·40	·00
r_{BB} ·6	·56	·43	·20	—
·5	·44	·29	·00	—

$r_{(A-B)\,(A-B)}$

In giving the Terman-Merrill scale, it is very tempting to interpret relative success or failure on different types of items as showing good or poor verbal ability, practical ability, immediate memory, etc., though McNemar (1942) discourages this practice. But the reliability of any one such item-type might be as low as 0·7, and its correlation with another item-type 0·5 or over; in which case discrepances between scores on the two types would have a reliability of less than 0·4. This would mean that a child who scored at, say, 8-year level on one type might well score at

---

[1] Cronbach (1949) provides a useful graph showing the proportions of score differences which are too large to be attributed to chance at various levels of reliability and inter-correlation. Table IV is based on the formula:

$$r_{(A-B)\,(A-B)} = \frac{\frac{1}{2}(r_{AA} + r_{BB}) - r_{AB}}{1 - r_{AB}}$$

6- or 10-year level on the other type by pure chance. The odds are only about 10 to 1 that he is genuinely superior or inferior.

Discrepancies between Verbal and Performance I.Q.s on the Wechsler scales are somewhat more trustworthy, their reliability approaching 0·7. But great caution is needed in interpreting scores on particular sub-tests which appear to be higher or lower than the testee's general level.

There has been much controversy also over I.Q.–E.Q. differences, which have traditionally been considered by British educational psychologists to show over- or under-achievement in school work. Often the ratio: $\frac{E.Q.}{I.Q.} \times 100$ or $\frac{E.A.}{M.A.} \times 100$ is calculated, and referred to as the *Achievement* or *Accomplishment Quotient*. Schonell, for example, distinguishes educational *backwardness*, where a child's attainment falls below his Chronological Age level, from educational *retardation*, where it falls below the level expected from his intelligence. Indeed, many educational psychologists tend to ignore the 'backward' on the grounds that little can be done for the innately dull and to concentrate their diagnostic and remedial efforts on the 'retarded'. Note that a child can be retarded, in this sense, even when his work is well up to the average of his age-group. If his average E.Q. is 110 but his I.Q. is 140, then his Achievement Quotient of 79 suggests that he is seriously 'under-functioning'.

Criticisms of this concept became widespread when it was pointed out that the distribution of A.Q.s would generally tend to be normal, i.e. there would be much the same numbers whose E.Q. exceeded as fell below their I.Q. How could children function 'above' their 'native capacity'? However, this difficulty merely reflects a misunderstanding of test norms. By definition the normal child must obtain the same E.A. as M.A. on well-standardised tests. And it is just as easy to envisage some children being superior in E.A. on account of specialised ability, or through good schooling, favourable environment or high persistence as it is to account for others falling below through lack of any of these qualities.

A more fundamental objection is the one we have put forward regarding reliability. If the reliability coefficients of intelligence and educational tests average 0·90 and their inter-correlation is 0·75, then the reliability of M.A.–E.A. differences is only 0·60.

Supposing we selected the 10 most retarded children in a group of 100, on the basis of one set of intelligence and educational tests, and then gave a second parallel set of tests, only 4 of the original 10 would again be diagnosed as highly retarded; the remaining 6 would be replaced by others who had previously been found to be only moderately retarded. In other words, the majority of low A.Q.s probably represent nothing more than chance differences.

A further objection arises on account of regression to the mean. Since the correlation between E.Q. and I.Q. falls below 1·0, the child of below average intelligence inevitably tends to do rather better at educational tests, and the above average one worse. In other words, it is very difficult for the high I.Q. child to work 'up to capacity' or for the low I.Q. one to work 'below capacity'. Again taking the 10 per cent of a group with lowest A.Q.s, it will be found that about twice as many with I.Q.s of 115 and over are included as of those with I.Q.s 85 or under. And if the correlation between I.Q. and E.Q. drops from 0·75 to 0·60 (as when a non-verbal group intelligence and a reading test are compared), the high I.Q. children diagnosed as retarded may outnumber the low I.Q. ones by 4 to 1.[1] Now, on general psychological grounds, we would expect to find 'under-functioning' more frequently among low I.Q. children, who more frequently come from homes unfavourable to education. Thus if we must contrast E.A. with M.A., we should at least make due allowance for regression (cf. Cureton, 1937).

Apart from all these statistical difficulties, we have already seen in Chapter II that it is fallacious to contrast intelligence as wholly inborn with attainment as wholly acquired. Indeed, psychologists in America banished the whole conception of the Achievement Quotient many years ago, and those in Britain would do well to follow them. We will take up again in the last chapter the question of the relevance of intelligence test performance to education.

USING TESTS FOR PREDICTION

The object of applying tests is to make predictions or decisions about people: that John is so backward in arithmetic that he will

[1] Such striking differences have not been noted in the literature on the subject, probably because the tests compared have seldom had really equivalent norms or standard deviations. A useful survey of the development of, and weaknesses in, the concept of the Achievement Quotient is provided by Crane (1959).

make no progress in school without remedial help, that Mary is sufficiently able to benefit from a grammar school education or to be suitable for a Civil Service job, that the distribution of reading ability in a given area calls for special measures to reduce illiteracy, and so on. A host of fresh problems arise at this point, and we can touch on them only briefly.

1. The validity of the test for the particular purpose is obviously crucial, and we have already seen that this may be difficult to establish (p. 46). Even in secondary school selection, for example, where it is generally quite straightforward to follow up pupils admitted to grammar schools, it is doubtful whether examination or other marks obtained after one or more years in the school provide an adequate criterion of 'benefiting from' this type of education (cf. Vernon, 1957). In the vocational field it is often found that the worker's satisfactoriness to his employers is almost unrelated to his own satisfaction with the career. Which of these criteria, then, should we try to predict?

2. It is seldom that one would expect a single test to provide all the information needed (except perhaps in establishing the degree or type of backwardness in the elementary stages of a school subject). Predictions are usually improved by including further tests of relevant qualities, though often less than we would anticipate. It is little use, for example, including educational attainment tests *and* scaled teachers' judgments in the 11-plus selection examinations, since they cover so much the same ground. And it is very doubtful policy adding an interview of the child, since subjective judgments are generally far less valid than are objective tests. The clinical or vocational psychologist likes to believe that he can build up a much more complete picture of a child's or adult's personality and abilities by combining information obtained from tests with personal data obtained by observation and interview, and that in this way he can predict the individual's reactions to various vocational careers, or to remedial or psychological treatment, and so on. This belief has been falsified in many researches which have shown better predictions from objective test data alone than from clinical judgments (cf. Vernon, 1953). The real advantage of the clinical, as against the statistical, approach is that it is far more flexible; it can take account of a wider variety of data which may be relevant only in individual cases, and suggest a much wider variety of treatments or other decisions

to suit such individuals than can a more objective selection pro-cedure. The disadvantage is that the clinical psychologist can only use his 'intuition' and 'experience' in deciding how much weight to attach to each of the relevant factors; whereas the statistical psychologist, in predicting some clear-cut outcome such as edu-cational or vocational success, can work out from his follow-up investigations just what weight should be given to each of his tests in order to produce maximum accuracy of prediction.

3. In any case, predictions should be regarded as actuarial, or possessing only a certain degree of probability. For example, we shall see in Chapter Ten that there are strong odds that a child with a high I.Q. will do well scholastically and vocationally, but we can never be certain whether any particular individual will not be an exception to this general trend. A large number ot influences not covered by the tests (nor by any other sources of information, such as the clinical interview) affect later success. Nevertheless, it is noteworthy that errors in prediction themselves tend to be distributed normally, i.e. there are a lot of small ones and fewer large discrepancies. Their extent depends, as we might expect, on the lowness of the correlation between the predicting test or tests and the criterion.

Within a group of pupils selected for grammar school, for example, the correlation between combined selection tests and later school grades is normally around 0·4 to 0·5. Suppose these school grades to be expressed in terms of marks ranging from about 90 down to 30 per cent. Then we are likely to find that the top third according to the selection tests will average about 10 per cent higher than those who were in the lowest third on ad-mission. But there will be so much variation that occasional good selectees may drop to a mark of 40 per cent, and occasional weak ones range up to 80 per cent. Just about one-quarter of the latter will get better marks than a quarter of the former.

4. Although tests such as those used in selection at 11-plus may not seem to be very efficient in predicting the exact degree of success within the selected group, their value may be much more apparent if we ask how well they separate the best 20 per cent of the age-group (or any other proportion) from the bottom 80 per cent. To estimate this, we can 'correct' the original correlations for 'homogeneity', and are likely to find that the correlation of 0·4 to 0·5 rises to 0·8 or over. This represents the agreement between the

tests and subsequent performance, had we been able to follow up the whole age-group (cf. Vernon, 1957).

The implication of such a correlation is that some two-thirds of those passing the selection tests do well later on, though one-third are less successful than an equal number of non-selectees would have been. As shown in Table V, 13 per cent are correctly selected and 73 per cent correctly rejected; but 14 per cent in all have been wrongly diagnosed.

TABLE V

ILLUSTRATING THE PROPORTIONS OF PUPILS
CORRECTLY SELECTED AT 11-PLUS

	Good performance later	Poor performance later	
Selected by tests .	13	7	20
Rejected by tests .	7	73	80
	20	80	100

Yates and Pidgeon (1957) and Vernon (1957) show that the efficiency of selection by a combination of tests and primary school teachers' estimates is represented by a correlation of 0·9 or over. But even this allows of some 10 per cent of mistaken allocations, since inevitably children's abilities change to some extent as they grow older and tackle new subjects in a new school.

5. The proportion of erroneous predictions depends not only on the level of correlation but on the *Selection Ratio*, that is the proportion of a population which is being chosen for a particular type of education or job. If the proportion is small, then even tests with quite low validity (0·2 to 0·4) may be of appreciable help in raising the quality of selected candidates, and thus reducing the proportions of failures. Similarly, at the bottom end of the scale a relatively invalid test will pick out a considerable proportion of the very weak, whereas when the Selection Ratio is large, there will be many more erroneously chosen unless the validity coefficient is very high. On the other hand the costs of testing in time, materials, etc., may become excessive when only a small number of individuals is to be chosen.

The complexity of conditions affecting the practical use of tests has been well brought out in a book by Cronbach and Gleser (1957). Sometimes a highly valid instrument like the intelligence test is less appropriate than a broader technique like the interview, or play-group observation, which provides leads or suggestions that can be followed up in individual cases. Again, the cumulative procedures of the classroom or the instructional group, where individuals are being diagnosed as their education or training proceeds, and their treatment accordingly adapted, may be more efficient than sectioning them once and for all into superior and inferior groups. Cronbach has gone some way to providing formulae for working out the most economic and efficient testing policy in various contexts.

6. Finally, further mention should be made of the difficult problem of differential prediction—deciding which of two or more types of schooling or job a person is best fitted for, or diagnosing to which of several clinical types he belongs. Though we may have two tests, each showing good validity in relation to one criterion (say, one of them valid for academic, the other for technical education), yet they may be of little use unless each shows a low correlation with the other criterion. Thus differential validity, like differential reliability (p. 119), implies a low correlation between the tests. Unfortunately, as we have seen, all tests of mental abilities are rather highly inter-correlated. There can be no doubt that more useful tests for educational, vocational and clinical purposes could be devised if this need for low correlations with other tests and other criteria were realised.

Chapter Eight

THE EFFECTS OF COACHING AND PRACTICE
ON INTELLIGENCE TESTS

THIS topic has assumed considerable importance since tests began to be applied on a large scale for selection, that is, in competitive situations where there are strong incentives to do well. Hence we shall discuss it at greater length than it probably deserves.[1]

As early as 1920 it was found, from experiments with the Army Alpha tests, that scores could be raised by an amount equivalent to some 5 I.Q. points simply by taking one previous parallel test; and it was soon shown that more intensive practice or coaching would lead to larger gains. But this hardly mattered so long as tests were chiefly employed in experimental investigations or for diagnostic purposes. In child guidance or vocational guidance, for example, the testee (or his parents) would have no desire to 'beat the test' or to obtain spuriously high scores. Provided, then, that the same or a similar test had not been taken at a recent date, the tester could afford to neglect possible practice or coaching. Moreover, individual Binet tests were the main instrument for individual diagnosis, and here the experienced tester can usually recognise previous acquaintance from the slickness of the testee's responses, or can cross-question him. (At the same time it is difficult to gauge how much allowance to make when such familiarity is discovered.)

But it is very different in group testing when the child's whole educational and subsequent vocational career, or the adult's job, may depend on the result, and when the tester cannot readily detect the incidence of coaching (apart from a rise in the average score for the whole group). Candidates, together with their parents and teachers, look on the intelligence test as another examination and naturally believe that coaching will give them a better chance of passing. The actual test to be used is generally kept secret, new ones being prepared every year. But most schools can get access to older, more or less parallel versions, and

[1] A fairly complete bibliography of published research may be found in the author's article (1954).

several publishers actually issue books of questions similar to those found in the standard tests. Many primary schools coach their pupils on these, even having Intelligence Tests as a subject on the time-table. Education Authorities generally prohibit or discourage this practice, but it is very difficult for teachers to hold out against parental pressure or against the temptation to secure as many passes as possible for their own school pupils. A large number of parents buy the commercial books for coaching at home, and some pay considerable fees to unscrupulous agencies that offer private coaching and imply that they can get any child 'through the 11-plus' for so many guineas.

Now that intelligence and other objective tests are generally included in the selection of Civil Servants and of officers and apprentices in the Defence Services, it is likely that coaching goes on for these as well, though we have no evidence so far that it is widespread. Doubtless the same thing would occur if tests began to be used for university entrance. But it is most serious among 10–11 year olds because of the atmosphere of strain that accompanies it and the inevitable distortions of good junior school education through over-concentration on training for the tests (cf. Vernon, 1957).

The layman is apt to blame the 11-plus examination as such, and particularly the intelligence test which he does not understand and therefore suspects, for this state of affairs. But clearly the fault lies with the system which demands a rigid separation of the 'wheat' from the 'chaff' at so early an age, and which provides for less than 10 per cent of 'wheat' in some areas, over 30 per cent in others; also with those parents who desire their children to have the cachet of attending a grammar school but who do little to encourage or help them once they are in the school, or who refuse to recognise that they may be unsuited to advanced academic education. Just as much stress and coaching would take place whatever the form of the examination itself, and we shall see below that intelligence tests are actually less coachable than other more conventional types of examination. It is quite absurd, therefore, just because psychologists have shown that coaching does produce rises in I.Q.s, to conclude that intelligence tests should forthwith be discarded.

Let us first distinguish various degrees or types of coaching:

A. Testees are taught the actual answers beforehand.

B. They have taken the same test one or more times before, but have not been told the right answers nor received other help.

C. Testees have taken similar tests before, without further instruction.

D. They have not taken a parallel test, but have been coached on more or less similar items—that is, told the right answers, had the underlying principles of the items explained, and given general hints on working carefully, not wasting time on difficult items, etc.

E. A combination of C + D, that is of practice *and* coaching.

Type A need not detain us: it does sometimes occur and, naturally, entirely upsets any test results.

B. PRACTICE ON THE IDENTICAL TEST

This is important, since children are often referred to an educational psychologist who does not know that they have been tested recently, or, if he does know, still wants to apply tests that lack alternative versions, such as WISC, Stanford-Binet or Collins-Drever performance tests. Repetition of verbal scales within a few months generally produces a rise of about 5 I.Q. points. Performance test batteries show just about twice this gain. Similarly, during World War II, Army and Navy psychologists had no parallels to their standard group tests, and recruits who were retested showed rises averaging 2·1 to 8·6 points for different tests. According to Heim's researches (1949–50), repeated retesting of adults at weekly intervals produces further almost indefinite rises, provided the test has sufficient 'headroom', though there is relatively little improvement beyond the fifth trial. On a test for 11-year olds, McIntosh (1944) obtained a mean gain of 7·2 points at the second trial, rising to 10·7 at the fifth, but there was a slight drop at the sixth.

Several significant points emerge from these and other researches.

1. The amount of improvement is limited; increased practice produces diminishing returns.

2. Although we have to quote *average* rises, there are great variations between individuals. With an average of 5 points, some testees gain up to 20 or more points and others actually lose as much as 10 points.

3. There are differences in improvability between different

tests. The research literature on this point is confusing, since gains in raw scores are usually reported, and these are quite non-comparable unless the tests have the same Standard Deviation. Here we have tried to reduce them to the same scale as that of Stanford-Binet and Moray House I.Q.s with a S.D. of 15. It would appear that the more complex and unfamiliar the test material and instructions, the greater the possibilities of improvement. The most straightforward tests like Vocabulary, Comprehension, Information and Creative Opposites generally yield the smallest rises; complicated Analogies, Abstraction and Classification tests, particularly those employing unfamiliar spatial or non-verbal material, are much more susceptible to improvement.

4. These practice effects are remarkably lasting. The evidence suggests that three-quarters of the gain found after one week is maintained up to six months, and half of it still remains after one year.

C. PRACTICE ON PARALLEL TESTS

Though the effectiveness of practice at other similar tests is smaller than that of practice at the identical test, it is still considerable. When Form M of Terman-Merrill is given shortly after Form L, the average gain is $2\frac{1}{2}$ points only. But in a typical group intelligence test the average gain from taking a single previous parallel version averages nearly 5 I.Q. points. Further practice tests produce smaller gains, totalling some 10 points after four or five tests. Thereafter the results are irregular, or the scores may decline, perhaps because the testees get bored. If children are already fairly sophisticated testees, the gains may be reduced to about half these amounts. Thus in a large-scale experiment with London children, Watts and others (1952) found the mean I.Q. on an eighth parallel test only 6 points higher than on the first. Several other factors besides previous familiarity may produce rather larger or smaller gains than those just quoted.

1. Age seems to make little difference. Adult recruits show very similar rises to 10-year children. Sex differences are sometimes reported, but do not consistently favour boys or girls.

2. The effects of the initial ability of the testees are difficult to evaluate, since the natural consequence of regression (p. 117) would be that below-average children would improve, and above-average ones decline on the second test. However, by

using initial + final score as a criterion, or by comparing per-centile levels, it is generally found that bright pupils (around I.Q. 120) gain about twice as much as dull ones (I.Q. 80). Peel (1951) claims that among still brighter ones (I.Q. 130 to 140+) the im-provement is less great. This might be attributed to lack of head-room in the test, but Peel considers that such children learn so easily on the first occasion that they have little room for later improvement.

3. When untimed and speeded versions of the same tests are compared, the rises are 75 to 90 per cent as great on the former as on the latter. Thus practice does not merely help in understanding instructions quickly. It is probable that the testees' learning of appropriate 'sets', i.e. methods of tackling the various types of items, together with the reduction of anxiety on the one hand and carelessness on the other, may be more important.

4. We have dealt already with the improvability of different kinds of tests. Comparisons have also been made between the omnibus and the battery types and no difference found (cf. p. 75n). What is important, though, is the degree of heterogeneity or diversity of types of items. Some battery tests such as Army Alpha and Otis Advanced give unusually big rises because they include such varied sub-tests, whereas Moray House tests are so constructed as to contain more homogeneous items. However, we should not avoid heterogeneous tests for this reason, since they are likely to be more valid in predicting future success than a narrower and more homogeneous instrument.

5. In the early days of group testing, Thorndike (1922) claimed that practice effects could be counteracted by making the test instructions clear and comprehensive and by providing adequate sample items or short practice exercises before the test started. This has been accepted by all test constructors, but more recent experi-ments with 11-year olds showed the conventional explanations and practice sheet to be totally ineffective. It was essential for children to do a complete test under examination conditions for the major practice effects to be overcome.

D. THE EFFECTIVENESS OF COACHING ON SIMILAR TEST MATERIALS

It is unfortunate that psychologists themselves have disagreed widely on this point and have thus confused teachers and the general public. Numerous experiments have yielded average gains of 15 or even 18 points of I.Q. after quite moderate amounts of coaching; others reported rises of only 5 or 6 points when fairly extensive coaching is given under ordinary school conditions, and it has even been stated that practice without instruction is as effective as, or more effective than, such coaching. However, a large amount of investigation has revealed the main reasons for these discrepant conclusions, and we can now generalise as follows: *coaching which includes practice at taking complete tests* (Type E) *does produce quite large gains*, whereas coaching carried out by teachers and parents from the items in published books, or on the basis of their own ingenuity, i.e. *coaching without practice is singularly ineffective, regardless of how protracted it is.* The other major factor is the testees' previous sophistication. Those who have had no previous experience of tests show rises about twice as large as those who have taken several educational or intelligence tests, or been coached at school, in the past. Thus, under present-day conditions, where the majority of British children (at least in urban areas) are to some extent 'test-wise', *the total average gain from taking two practice tests + a few hours of interspersed coaching is* not 5 or 15 but *about 9 points.* This is confirmed, not just by small-scale experiments but by practical trials including complete 11-year age-groups in large boroughs. With similar children, a single practice test gives only 3-4 points, and several practices 5-6 points. Thus coaching does add something, but remarkably little, and obviously far less than teaching does in the case of ordinary school examinations. As always, there are a number of other relevant factors to be considered.

1. Big individual differences in 'coach-ability' are found. Thus some 14 per cent of children gain from 15 up to 25 or more points, while some 5 per cent show no gain at all, or even lose despite all that coaching and practice can achieve. In most Education Areas also, there will always be some children (e.g. from private or from remote rural schools) who have no previous experience of tests at all, and they are likely to be handicapped much more seriously—by an average of 12 or more points—in comparison with fully coached children.

The differences were also emphasised by Watts (1952) in his detailed study of the progress of pupils who took 10 successive tests with interspersed coaching. While there was no appreciable average improvement beyond the fifth test, some children reached their maximum earlier, some later. Some then remained steady, others fluctuated considerably.

2. The maximum effects of coaching are achieved very quickly, and teachers, parents or others who carry out larger amounts are more likely to produce falls than further rises. Watts reports two experiments comparing groups coached for 3, 6 and 9 hours. At the end the 6-hour groups were distinctly poorer than the 3-hour; the 9-hour recovered slightly but did not surpass the 3-hour.

3. The effects of coaching and practice tend to be highly specific, i.e. there is relatively little transfer to other types of test items or to different testing conditions. Thus we have already seen that coaching without practice under examination conditions yields very poor gains. In one experiment, no effect on Verbal Analogies and Classification could be discovered from coaching on Non-verbal Analogies and Classification, nor vice versa. Indeed, there is evidence that experience at one type of test sometimes decreases ability at other dissimilar types. When a battery of several diverse tests is applied, it is found that the average scores vary slightly (1 or 2 per cent only) according to the order in which the tests are done. This must mean that the 'set' or method of work appropriate to any one test helps the adjustment to some of the succeeding tests and hinders it to others. The type of coaching which parents carry out from books of items is likely to be very ineffective because both the methods of work and some of the types of items are too unlike the actual selection test.

At the same time, people can and do develop a degree of sophistication to tests in general, through coaching and particularly through practice. They learn to avoid over-excitement and anxiety, to work quickly and not waste time on difficult items, but to take careful account of instructions, and so on. American pupils and students are likely to be more sophisticated than British in this sense, partly because so many of their school examinations are new-type, that is, couched in the same form as standardised tests. But even American students are found to do intelligence tests better at college according as they have taken 1, 2, 3 or more different intelligence tests previously. The present writer showed in 1938 that a short course of lectures on mental tests, including the taking of illustrative tests, raised the average level of students on dissimilar tests by 4 I.Q. points. In the Scottish Research

Council's surveys of intelligence at 11 years, children in 1947 who lived in urban areas where they were likely to become familiar with tests showed a rise of 3·2 points over 1932, whereas those in more remote areas, where tests were still little used, showed a rise of only 0·4 points. Again, the Moray House organisation has found the British norms for its intelligence tests to rise from 1945 to 1955, till now they seem to have become stabilised at a level 6 points above pre-war (Pilliner, 1959). In other words, the present-day test-sophisticated child with an I.Q. of 100 on current tests scores I.Q. 106 on parallel pre-war tests. Of course, this may represent a genuine rise due to improved education, health and social conditions, but an explanation in terms of test-familiarity seems more plausible.

4. It is extremely likely that some teachers are more effective coaches than others, though it has been difficult to prove this because of the large random variations that occur in the gains of one child, or one class of children, as compared with another. We cannot specify, either, what constitute successful or unsuccessful coaching methods; probably they are much the same as good and poor teaching methods in general.

5. The effects of coaching seem to fade more rapidly than those of practice, though there is a paucity of evidence. In one experiment a group tested 2 months after coaching showed only two-thirds the gain of a group tested 1½ weeks after. The following results, adapted from Greene's study (1928) of the Stanford-Binet, are interesting.

TABLE VI

EFFECTS OF COACHING ON STANFORD-BINET I.Q.s

| | Mean Gain when Retested after: | | | |
	3 wks.	3 mths.	1 yr.	3 yrs.
Children coached on test itself . .	29·1	17·5	12·6	4·3
Coached on similar test material .	7·9	7·6	5·6	1·5
Control children, not coached . .	5·0	2·6	3·3	0·6

Several small groups of children were coached either on the actual test items or on similar ones, and retested after varying intervals. Controls were not coached, but nevertheless showed some average rise as a result of taking the test before. Here both the coaching on similar material and the practice effect (in the control group) are still quite strong after one year, though the coaching on the test itself has faded. They do not wear off completely until, after three years, the children have progressed to quite a different part of the scale. This suggests that insufficient account has been taken of practice effects in some of the investigations of environmental influences on intelligence (cf. Chapter Nine).

6. Age and sex of the testees make no consistent difference. The influence of initial ability is also uncertain, but with practice *and* coaching the moderately bright still tend to gain most. This means, incidentally, that improvability is greatest round about the borderline level for selection. Those with I.Q.s 115–120 can gain an average of 11–12 points instead of the 9 points quoted above.

7. The types of test item most susceptible to improvement through practice also seem to be the most coachable.

DISCUSSION

It is sometimes claimed that the liability of intelligence tests to practice or coaching matters less at the 11-plus selection stage because intelligence carries only part of the weight. If combined with English and arithmetic, for example, a 9-point gain would represent only 3 points gain in the average for all three tests. However, this is fallacious since the English and arithmetic tests probably offer at least as much scope for coaching. That is to say, children can gain not only in their knowledge of these subjects as such, but also in their facility at taking educational tests, in their confidence and carefulness, and in methods of work. A conservative estimate of the total difference between coached + practised and inexperienced candidates at the selection examination would be 22 points of I.Q. + En.Q. + Ar.Q. If the borderline were fixed to select 20 per cent of pupils and if half were effectively coached, half not, then some 30 per cent of the coached and 10 per cent of the unsophisticated pupils would achieve success. The present writer, testing in a county area, has found candidates from small rural schools markedly inferior in reading comprehension items and speed of mechanical arithmetic—that is, in material of the type likely to be practised by many larger urban schools—though the equal of the town children in vocabulary and spelling, that is, in some of the basic skills needed for grammar school work.

While it is clear, then, that coaching + practice effects are large enough to make a considerable difference in selection, it is equally true that 'intelligence' cannot be taught in at all the same sense as are school subjects. The total increase is limited and there is no continued improvement with continued training. We have shown, too, that the effects tend to be specific; in other words, training in intelligence tests probably does nothing to increase intelligence at anything else. Even the general sophistication effect merely means familiarity with the kinds of items and methods of work appropriate to most psychological tests. In a later chapter we shall see that some types of school curriculum and some teachers probably do help to stimulate the growth of all-round intelligence. This is to be welcomed; and the consequent increase that it brings in intelligence test scores is wholly legitimate. But a type of instruction which concentrates merely on increasing test scores is equally to be deplored.

What can be done to counteract it? If coaching and practice were wholly specific in their effects, it would be sufficient to devise new types of test on each occasion. But we have seen that there is quite a considerable general element. Moreover, the ingenuity of test constructors is not unlimited, and it would be extremely expensive and time-consuming to carry out the necessary experimental trials of novel tests; they would seldom be as reliable or valid as the already established varieties. Certainly some alternation of types of test, and greater use of those types which are known to be less coachable,[1] would help to reduce the present unfairness, but would do nothing to reduce the pressure on the children and the waste of time on coaching at school or at home.

Now injustices arise in so far as some candidates have been coached or practised, others not. When all candidates have been coached, the selection borderline has to be raised and the test norms altered, but no one is unfairly handicapped. It is the existence of 'differential' coaching of some children and not of others that really matters. Hence one solution is to authorise teachers in all primary schools to give coaching and practice. This is all the more

[1] Travers (1938) has suggested an attractive alternative. By including some relatively coachable types of items, others less coachable, it would be possible to determine statistically, which children, or which schools, had received coaching. Unfortunately, the technique is too complicated and seems too unreliable for practical application.

plausible since so little training is needed to bring about maximal improvement. Candidates who had received additional illicit coaching would gain no further advantage; they might even do worse than those who had the small amount of legitimate training. It would also have the positive advantage of showing all children what the selection examination was going to be like, and thus helping to reduce their anxieties. The precise amount of coaching required should be decided in the light of local conditions. In areas where grammar school provision is lavish, where coaching is still fairly rare, and where adequate use is made of primary teachers' estimates or of other criteria besides competitive tests, it would probably be sufficient to provide all children with a single trial run, plus an hour or so's instruction based on their scripts. This trial should include all the selection tests, not the intelligence test only. But in areas where competition is more severe and coaching widespread, and where selection is based solely on objective tests, it would be desirable to allow two parallel trials, to mark the tests in class and to allow teachers to give further guidance for a few periods after each trial. The teachers should also be supplied with hints on effective coaching, and every opportunity should be taken to inform teachers and parents of the harmfulness and futility of coaching beyond the limited amount. Analogous steps seem to be required in other competitive testing situations, such as selection for the Civil Service.

One objection that has been raised to this solution is that, if teachers vary in their effectiveness as coaches, it would reintroduce big differences between the performances of different school classes. While there is some truth in this, the differences would still not be so large as those existing at present when some classes are thoroughly coached and others have no previous acquaintance with tests at all. Another practical query concerns the effects on the reliability and validity of the examination. If, as Watts has shown, children vary so much in the gains they make, what justification is there for assuming that post-coaching scores give any better indication of future educability than pre-coaching ones? Watts suggests that a combination of the results of several tests given at different stages of familiarisation would provide the best estimates.

It is indeed generally true that two or more tests (or sets of tests) are more reliable and valid than one. But the principle hardly applies if the results of the first test are distorted by some children having had a good deal of previous experience, others none. In these circumstances the later tests, when all children have had some experience, are likely to be more trustworthy.

Curious as it may seem, the effects of coaching on reliability and validity are so small that it is difficult for the psychometrist to determine which tests are most predictive. If we take an extreme case where half the candidates are coached and show an average rise of 22 points of I.Q. + En.Q. + Ar.Q., half have had none, the consequence is only a 3 per cent reduction in the correlation co-efficients. If the normal correlation with subsequent secondary school success is 0·85, the correlation under these abnormal conditions would still be 0·825. This emphasises the point already made that the susceptibility of tests to coaching and practice, and the unfairness that this produces in individual cases near the border-line, does not imply that tests become useless.

Our plan would have the disadvantage of upsetting the norms for published group tests. But they are already rendered inapplic-able through the existence of widespread illicit coaching. For-tunately, it would have little effect on performance in most of the individual intelligence and attainment tests which the educational psychologist uses in studying backward or maladjusted children. Research investigations and surveys of children over the 10–12-year age-range would also be affected by universal coaching, though certainly no worse than they are at present by differential coaching. Actually, the controversies over coaching have been beneficial in bringing home to psychologists that previous ex-perience of tests does make a difference and must be allowed for in drawing any conclusions.

In the long run, however, no entirely satisfactory solution can be expected through modifications of testing technique and ad-ministration. So long as tests are misused for competitive pur-poses, as distinct from diagnostic and research purposes, the problem will continue. If secondary school selection became a process of allocation, as the 1944 Act envisaged, and if this allocation were a continuing process, reflecting children's needs and abilities throughout their school careers instead of being based on one set of examinations at 11, the incentives to coach would disappear.

Chapter Nine

HEREDITY AND ENVIRONMENT

WE have seen that the intelligence which can be observed in daily life, or which is measured by our tests, should not be identified with pure inborn native capacity nor regarded as something sharply distinguished from knowledge or skills acquired through upbringing and education. Nevertheless, there are still wide divergences of view as to the relative importance of nature and nurture, and much controversy over the interpretation of the relevant evidence. Psychologists such as Terman, Burt and R. B. Cattell have consistently maintained that the intelligence we measure is mainly determined by the genes and that the influence of environment is quite small. Others go to the opposite extreme. J. B. Watson, the Behaviourist, claimed to be able to produce any type of man, talented or otherwise, by training him from birth; and many American writers, notably the Iowa school of educational psychologists and the Chicago sociologists, would appear to deny any role to heredity.

The psychologists just mentioned are all serious scientists who strive to maintain impartiality of outlook. But only too often people's views on this topic are distorted by political and other prejudices. Those with left-wing opinions dislike the assumption that anyone born from an upper- or middle-class family has some innate superiority over those of less privileged birth, and believe that social reform and improved education will rectify such divergences. Whereas the view often expressed in the nineteenth century, and still occasionally heard, is that the poor cannot benefit from, and do not deserve, as good an environment and education as the rich. Communist theory so strongly emphasises the modifiability of genetic constitution that for a time Mendelian principles were rejected in Soviet Russia, and intelligence testing is still regarded merely as a ruse to perpetuate social-class and educational differences. The most extreme hereditarians were the Nazi racial theorists of the 1930s, who ascribed all the desirable human traits and abilities to people of Nordic descent, all the undesirable ones to Jews. German psychology and biology became as perverted (in the opposite direction) as Russian is today. Thus a highly reputable pre-war German psychologist, E. Jaensch, descended to such nonsense as: "The superiority of Nordic races is reflected in race differences among chickens. The Nordic chick is better behaved and more efficient in feeding than the Mediterranean chick, and less apt to over-eat by suggestion. These differences parallel certain temperamental differences among humans. The poultry-yard confutes the liberal-Bolshevik claim that race differences are merely cultural differences, because race differences among chicks cannot be accounted for by culture."

The conclusions reached in this book are middle-of-the-road. They allow considerably more scope to the influence of upbringing than do most previous books by British psychologists. Yet they will not please the left-wing theorist, since they recognise that there is clear evidence for some hereditary determination. Several different lines of enquiry have been very extensively explored, and we will proceed to survey their findings in turn.

PEDIGREE STUDIES

Sir Francis Galton led the way with his studies of 'hereditary genius'. In his own family and that of the related Huxleys and Darwins there was a remarkable galaxy of talent, suggesting that ability is passed from one generation to another. On making a systematic study of nearly one thousand men of acknowledged eminence, he found that a large proportion of their close relatives were also outstanding—far more than in the general population. At the opposite end of the scale the most famous pedigrees to be worked out are those of the Kallikak family and the Jukes. Though these are of little scientific value, a summary of the latter may be of some interest. Mr. Jukes, born about 1830 in North America, was a hunter and a fisher, whose sons married into a degenerate family of sisters. One hundred and eighty years later information was collected on some 2,000 descendants. Of these, 378 died in infancy and 301 were illegitimate; 366 were paupers, 80 habitual thieves, 171 convicted of other crimes, including 10 murders; 175 were prostitutes and 55 with venereal disease had infected 600 other persons. In 1915, out of 1,258 living descendants, about half the adults were fair or good citizens; nearly as many were 'antisocial', and 103 were 'marked cases of mental defect'. Between 1800 and 1915 they had cost the State $2\frac{1}{2}$ million dollars.

Now, even apart from the obvious difficulties of assessing the traits and abilities of people long dead, such studies are of little or no scientific value, since the findings could equally well be accounted for by the cultural intellectual environment in which the Galtons and their like were brought up and the depressing immoral environment of the Jukes. Indeed, before long, studies similar to Galton's were published by De Candolle in France and J. McK. Cattell in America claiming just the opposite conclusion. They showed that eminent men of science came most frequently from the rich and leisured classes, in countries (or parts of the U.S.A.) where there was a good system of education, plentiful libraries and laboratories, freedom of opinion and absence of religious censorship. One might, of course, answer that families with high talents were more likely to settle in such environments and to continue improving the conditions rather than that the conditions improved them. But such arguments regarding cause and effect would be fruitless.

CORRELATIONS BETWEEN INTELLIGENCE OF OFFSPRING AND INTELLIGENCE OR OCCUPATIONAL STATUS OF PARENTS

Turning to more modern work, it is obviously preferable to compare objective measurements of intelligence rather than subjective estimates of ability. It is not easy to persuade parents of tested children to take tests themselves, but Conrad and Jones (1940) succeeded in applying the Stanford-Binet to all the children and Army Alpha to the adults in a representative sample of families in an area in New England. They obtained an average correlation of 0·49. Many other studies yield a correlation around 0·5 between siblings (i.e. ordinary brothers and sisters), and one would expect the genetic resemblance of parent-offspring or of two offspring in one family to be the same.[1] Conrad and Jones noted that mother–child correlations were no higher than father–child, nor like-sex higher than unlike-sex, as might have been anticipated on environmentalist theories. Moreover, the co-

[1] R. B. Cattell points out that, after allowing for test unreliability, the correlation of the average of the children with the average of their parents may be as high as 0·8. Even this figure would permit quite a wide range of variation between child and parent intelligence, as would indeed be expected on theories of determination by multiple genes.

efficient is much the same as that for height, which is an attribute known to be largely dependent on heredity.

Another approach is to test the relatives of mentally defective persons who, even though they are certified on other grounds besides low intelligence, do usually fall below I.Q. 70. Both Burt (1955a) and Penrose (1938) have found that only about 14 per cent of the children of an adult defective are themselves defective or obtain I.Q.s below 70. Just about the same proportions obtain I.Q.s of 100 and over. This regression to the mean is just what would be expected from a parent-child correlation of 0·5. It is equally true that many parents of normal intelligence have children who fall within the defective range, and that the majority of defective children are born of dull (around I.Q. 85) rather than of defective parents. However, Penrose, Fraser Roberts (1952) and others have pointed out that the abilities of relatives of low-grade defectives differ markedly from those of the relatively high-grade. The parents and siblings of imbeciles and idiots are not predominantly dull, but tend either to be defective themselves or else normal or superior. Now when a defective child occurs in a defective or dull family, we can usually explain this by means of the ordinary processes of inheritance coupled with upbringing in an inferior environment. But when an imbecile is born in a good family there is likely to be some accidental or pathological cause, such as gene mutations, prenatal uterine conditions or (as in the case of cretins) glandular defects in the mother, or birth injury or brain disease. No hard-and-fast distinction can be drawn between types, since the causation of mental deficiency is so often multiple, i.e. genetic, intrauterine, environmental and pathological (cf. Clarke, 1958). But the existence of the latter, so-called exogenous type, in addition to the former endogenous type, does help to account for the peculiar discrepancies between parental and child ability in the case of low-grades. It also explains why there seem to be more defectives, especially low-grades, in the total population than would be expected if intelligence were strictly normally distributed (cf. p. 110).

Partly because of the difficulties of testing parents, and partly because of the intrinsic interest of parental occupational status, the relation of the latter to child intelligence has been more fully studied. In Thomson's first survey in Northumberland, the mean I.Q.s of the children of over 100 occupational groups were obtained, of which the following are examples (Duff and Thomson, 1923):

Clergymen	121
Total professional	112
Commercial and business	105–110
Industrial workers	100–103
Labourers and agriculture	96–98
Hawkers and chimney sweeps	91

Similarly, Terman and Merrill (1937), in standardising the revised Stanford-Binet scale, obtained the figures shown in Table VII.

TABLE VII

PARENTAL OCCUPATIONAL DISTRIBUTION AND
TERMAN-MERRILL I.Q.s OF CHILDREN

Occupational Group	Father's Occupation	Per cent of Sample	Mean I.Q. of Children
I	Professional	5	116
II	Semi-professional and managerial .	8	112
III	Clerical, skilled trades, retail business	26	107
V	Semi-skilled, minor clerical and business	31	105
VI	Slightly skilled	9	98
IV and VII	Rural and day labourers . .	22	95

Though a different classification was used in the 1947 Scottish Mental Survey, the trend of results was much the same. Indeed, one can generalise that children of the upper professional groups usually score 1 Standard Deviation above the mean, and those of the least skilled labouring groups ½ a Standard Deviation below. The latter do not fall so far below as the former rise above the mean because they constitute so much larger a proportion of the total population.

Note that here again there is regression towards the mean. The highest and lowest groups of fathers would be likely to score 2 S.D. above and 1 S.D. below the mean. We should also realise that there is tremendous overlapping. A few labourers' children will range up to 130+ I.Q. and a few professional children down to 80 or less (in addition to 'freak' defectives). As Gray and Moshinski have stressed (1936), the greatest absolute numbers of very bright children come from occupational groups III and V, i.e. from the working class, clerical and retail fathers. The professional and upper business parents produce the biggest *relative proportion* but a smaller *total* of the outstanding intelligences of the next generation. Hence the necessity (whether we incline either to hereditarian or environmental theories) for the educational system to promote social mobility by allowing the brightest children to come to the top regardless of their origins.

The correlation of father's occupational level with child's I.Q. is consistently found to be about 0·35; that is, a little lower than the correlation for parent's intelligence (cf. Fleming, 1943). But with tests such as Gesell's, given to 0–6-month infants, parental class correlates zero or slightly negatively; the higher-class child is, if anything, slightly poorer in early sensory-motor development. The relationship becomes increasingly positive from 1 to 4 years, as the tests become more conceptual and verbal in content. This does not necessarily show the increasing effects of environment between 0 and 4; it would be equally plausible to say that the genes underlying intelligence do not come into operation until the higher brain-centres mature.

Now, although all the findings so far quoted are consistent with genetic determination, they could equally well be explained through the better upbringing that high-intelligence or high social-class parents can provide than lower ones, their richer vocabulary, more favourable attitudes to schooling, etc. Indeed, the Chicago sociologists, Davis, Havighurst and Eells (Eells *et al.*, 1951), take precisely this view. They find that middle-class children do better than working-class even on spatial and non-verbal intelligence test items, though particularly on vocabulary items. By 10 years the difference between the highest and lowest socio-economic groups amounts to 4 years of Vocabulary M.A. And they interpret this to mean that the tests largely measure training in middle-class linguistic culture. They have attempted to construct a series of 'culture-free' tests, but so far apparently without much success.[1] While their work provides a valuable new slant on cultural differences between classes in child-rearing

---

[1] The Davis-Eells Games test, based mainly on comprehension of comic-strip pictures which are applied orally, still tends to show class differences.

practices, which might well affect intellectual development, it
ignores the possibility that class differences in intelligence might
be to some extent innate.[1]

The trouble is, of course, that children's environment is usually
of a piece with their heredity. The more innately intelligent
parents, who pass on superior genes, also tend to provide the best
environment; hence the difficulty of separating the contributions
of nature and nurture. One of the few really conclusive investigations which did manage to do this is that of Lawrence (1931),
who measured the intelligence of illegitimate orphans. These
children had had no contact with the fathers, and had been
separated from their mothers before the age of 6 months. However, the occupations of the fathers were known, and there was
still a correlation of about 0·25 with the child's I.Q. This provides
definite confirmation of genetic class differences. But equally, in
so far as it is lower than the figure of about 0·35 for children
brought up by their own parents, it proves the influence of
environment.

Further very strong evidence is provided, not by the moderate
resemblance between children and parents or between siblings, but
by the *differences*. On genetic theory, the reshuffling of parental
genes at each conception would be expected to produce quite a
wide range of intelligence in the same family, whereas it would be
much more difficult to explain this on environmental theory.
Parents do of course often favour, or pay more attention to, one
child than another, though not necessarily the one who turns out
the brightest. Such favouritism could hardly bring about differences of 30 to 40 I.Q. points. Thus the fact that professors occasionally have very dull children, or unskilled labourers very bright
ones, points inevitably to the importance of hereditary factors.

Likewise we observe even larger differences between orphans,
although they are reared in highly standardised institutional environments. The uniformity of their upbringing may have had
some effect, but it does not seem to make them much more
homogeneous in I.Q. than children brought up in more varied
environments. Another argument that school teachers might
bring forward is that huge differences in mentality persist between
the children in their classes despite all their efforts. However, anti-

[1] This possibility is sometimes disputed by British sociologists also (Halsey,
1958).

hereditarians could answer here that such differences are firmly fixed by the much more pervasive influence of upbringing outside the school.

One further point should be made: though we have admitted that the environment affects the child's intelligence, we should not forget that the child's intelligence often affects the environment. Parents who find one of their children showing greater intellectual promise than another are likely to provide the former with more books and other intellectual stimulation. He is also likely to get into higher junior school streams and to win a grammar school place and this, as we shall see later, may still further widen the gap between him and the less gifted.

STUDIES OF TWINS

Identical or monozygotic twins are produced by the division of the mother's ovum after it has been fertilised by the father's sperm. Thus they possess the same genes and the same hereditary potentialities. Fraternal or dizygotic twins, like ordinary siblings, grow from separately fertilised ova. Hence there are even chances that they will be of the same or opposite sex, whereas identicals are always like-sex. Again, if one of them receives parental genes underlying high intelligence there are even chances that the other member of a pair will, or will not, do so. Among more distant relatives such as two first cousins, or a grandparent and grandchild, the hereditary resemblance is halved again, i.e. there is a one-in-four chance of any gene being present in both.

Now on correlating the intelligence test results of pairs, a typical result is:

Identical twins	0·90
Fraternal like-sex	0·70
Fraternal unlike-sex	0·60
Siblings	0·50
First cousins	0·27
Unrelated children	0·00

The resemblance of identicals is almost as high as the reliability of the tests employed, i.e. as high as the correlation of one child's I.Q. with his own I.Q. on a parallel test. As hereditary resemblance decreases, so does the correlation, and this fact is usually quoted as strong evidence for the inheritance of intelligence. But it will be noted that fraternal twins, especially like-sex ones, correlate more highly than siblings, which they should not, since their genetic resemblance is the same.[1] Further, any closer correlation between identicals than fraternals could plausibly be attributed to greater similarity of environment. Identicals are usually dressed alike and treated alike; and qualitative studies show that they seem to have a peculiar bond of sympathy with one another, always doing things together and sharing the same interests. Fraternals, however, are more often rivals at home and at school, and quarrel as much as siblings habitually do.

A crucial test is provided by identicals brought up in different environments. Naturally these are rare, but Newman, Freeman and Holzinger (1937) traced 19 pairs in America who had been separated at an early age, and Burt (1955) has tested 21 others. In Newman's research the median difference in Stanford-Binet I.Q. was $7\frac{1}{2}$ instead of the 5 points normally found for pairs brought up together, and a few pairs showed differences ranging up to 20 points. Moreover, the greater the discrepancy in cultural level of the two homes, on the whole the greater the differences in I.Q. The authors conclude that differences attributable to environment are about as large as differences due to heredity, but this is denied by other psychometrists who have analysed their data. Perhaps the neatest analysis of twin and sibling data is that published by Shuttleworth (1935), who concludes that differences in children's intelligence may be attributed approximately as follows:

64 per cent to hereditary factors;

15 per cent to environmental differences between families;

3 per cent to differences in upbringing between children in the same family;

18 per cent to joint hereditary-environmental contributions, i.e. to the fact that families with good heredity usually also provide superior environments.

This conclusion is reasonably consonant with that reached by other writers, such as Burt in England and Burks in America, and it brings out the point that one cannot really separate nature from nurture; they interact with one another from conception onwards. However, Burt's method of analysis yields a somewhat higher weight to heredity. He bases it on the following correla-

---

[1] A partial explanation is that fraternals are tested at the same age, siblings at least a year apart; thus the tests used are more closely similar for the former.

tions for his own groups of twins (the corresponding figures from Newman's research are added in brackets). These show that the resemblance in intelligence between identicals reared apart is far higher than the resemblance between unrelated children brought

TABLE VIII

BURT'S AND NEWMAN'S CORRELATIONS BETWEEN
PAIRS OF TWINS, SIBLINGS AND UNRELATED CHILDREN

Type of Relationship	Height	Intelligence (Indiv. Test)	General Attainments
Identicals reared together .	·957 (·981)	·921 (·910)	·898 (·955)
Identicals reared apart .	·951 (·969)	·843 (·670)	·681 (·507)
Fraternals reared together .	·472 (·930)	·526 (·640)	·831 (·883)
Siblings reared together .	·503	·491	·814
Unrelated children in same home . . .	—·069	·252	·535

up together; whereas in the case of school attainments the correlation of 0·535 attributable to the same environment with different heredity is much more nearly equal to that of 0·681 for the same heredity with different environment. From these figures Burt claims that the contribution of heredity to individual differences in intelligence amounts to 83 per cent, in height 92 per cent and attainments 40 per cent. But correlations for small numbers are, of course, unstable; and, applying the same method of analysis to Newman's data yields: intelligence 75 per cent, height 73 per cent, attainments 62 per cent. This would support our claim, in Chapter Two, that there is little essential difference between intelligence and attainments.

CONSTANCY OF THE I.Q. AND OF ATTAINMENTS

If it were true that intelligence test results depended almost wholly on innate ability, the I.Q. would be expected to remain constant throughout life. We have already seen that the degree of constancy is fairly high over short periods, much less so over long ones, though also that much of this variability may be due to imperfections in the tests and only part of it to alterations in the testees.

Interestingly enough, the degree of fluctuation does not seem to be very different for school attainments. For though we tend to think of pupils as rising or falling considerably in their school performance in successive classes, this is more true of marks in particular subjects than of all-round success; and here, too, much of the variation arises from the unreliability of school examinations. In one investigation of some 1,200 pupils in 19 primary schools, Blandford (1958) found somewhat higher correlations between Attainment Quotients over $2\frac{1}{2}$ years than between Intelligence Quotients.[1] It is likely, of course, that greater alterations in attainment may occur when children change schools and advance to new or more complex school subjects—hence the value of intelligence tests at the end of the junior school in predicting secondary school performance. But we certainly cannot claim that intelligence remains entirely stable or that attainments are wholly at the mercy of environment.

We will now ask how far changes in intelligence have been shown to result from particular environmental conditions.

EFFECTS OF UNUSUAL ENVIRONMENTS

In 1923 Gordon published a study of canal boat and gipsy children who had very little if any schooling. On the Binet test they were of nearly average intelligence up to the age of 6, but thereafter their M.A.s failed to progress at the normal rate as lack of schooling made itself felt, and their I.Q.s consequently dropped. On performance tests there was no such marked difference. This was taken to mean, not so much that intelligence is affected by schooling, as that a verbal test such as Binet cannot legitimately be used unless children have had normal educational opportunities. Similar findings have been reported from isolated communities in the United States. A recent study by Weil in Brazil showed that non-verbal ability (on a test similar to Matrices) may be affected as much as verbal ability. He tested some 27,000 persons from 6 to 60 years, many of whom had had no schooling whatever. The scores in illiterate communities up to 6 years were normal, but thereafter there was practically no increase whatever.

Another interesting British investigation was that of Dawson

---

[1] This unexpected finding may be due partly to the greater reliability of the attainment tests than the intelligence test; the former took several hours to give, the latter only half an hour.

(1936) on slum clearance. Over two hundred 5–8-year children were tested in a poor and overcrowded part of Glasgow, shortly before they moved to a new housing estate. On retesting after 1 to $1\frac{1}{2}$ years in the new environment they showed a small, but statistically significant, increase of $1\frac{1}{2}$ I.Q. points, whereas a control group that stayed behind showed no significant improvement. It is perhaps surprising that the newer schools and the more healthy and stimulating environment could have even as much effect as this in a relatively short period.

Some of the most extensive enquiries have dealt with foster children. F. N. Freeman tested brothers and sisters (who could be regarded as potentially of the same *average* intelligence), some of whom were placed in good and intellectually stimulating homes, others in poorer homes. The estimated effect of the difference attributable to such different environments was 10 to 20 points of I.Q. This may not sound very large, but the correlation between siblings in different homes fell from the usual figure of 0·50 to 0·25; moreover, a higher correlation, namely 0·37, was obtained for unrelated foster children in the same home. These findings were criticised on the grounds that the more intelligent and better-class foster parents would tend to take more trouble in selecting bright children for adoption. Other similar studies by Burks and Leahy confirmed the existence of selective placement, and provided additional evidence that the environmental influence of the foster-home on the child's I.Q. is limited.[1]

From 1938 on, a series of studies were issued by Wellman, Skeels and Skodak at Iowa University, purporting to show far greater effects of altered environment on the I.Q. For example, it was claimed that 26 children, whose mean I.Q. at 3 years was 90, were sent to an orphanage where there was an extreme lack of intellectual stimulus, no play materials, and an uneducated nurse in charge. When retested 2 years later the mean I.Q. had dropped to 74, and many of the children fell below the borderline for mental deficiency. On the other hand, a group of illegitimate children of subnormal mothers (said to average I.Q. 88), who had been placed in good foster homes, were found to obtain a mean

---

[1] The work on foster children, together with the Iowa studies and other relevant investigations, is summarised in the 27th and 39th *Yearbooks* of the National Society for the Study of Education (Bloomington, Ill.: Public School Publishing Co., 1928 and 1940).

I.Q. of 116, that is 28 points higher. Skeels actually concludes that when people adopt young children there is no point in their enquiring into the children's heredity. Other investigations dealt with nursery school attendance. Thus it was claimed that I.Q.s tend to rise from September to April when children are attending such schools but not during April to September, which is mostly holiday. It was even found that university students who many years before had attended nursery schools, did better on intelligence tests than those who had not.

Such assertions were naturally challenged, particularly by followers of Terman (McNemar, 1940). The Iowa investigators do not seem to have used proper controls, and were sometimes careless in their choice of tests and in their statistical methods and calculations. Variations in the norms of tests for young children were ignored. The favourable effects of nursery school attendance (which are not confirmed by other more scientifically planned studies) might be due to the dependence of the tests on play materials such as are freely used in such schools, or else to better emotional adjustment to social situations such as taking a test. If there were any superiority in the ex-nursery school students, this might arise from greater test sophistication, i.e. to their being tested more frequently from nursery school onwards. Reworking of the orphan and foster-home data, it is claimed, points to environmental effects of the order of 5 to 10 points—much the same as Freeman and others found—rather than 20 to 30 points.

CHANGES AMONG MENTAL DEFECTIVES

The diagnosis and treatment of mental defect has traditionally been the province of the medical profession, with the result that the mental defective has been considered as someone suffering from an incurable brain defect. More exact study by psychological methods, however, has shown that defectives are just as liable as normals to vary in intelligence when retested, and that their intellectual and personality development is affected in much the same way by emotional factors or adverse environmental conditions. Thus the fact that a child is found to have an I.Q. below 70 and is transferred to a special, or E.S.N., school gives little indication of what sort of adult he will become. Follow-up studies of such children in America by Baller (1936) and Charles (1953) showed that less than 7 per cent were in institutions for feeble-minded adults. Over 80 per cent became at least partially self-supporting in jobs which, while mostly low-grade, did range quite high up the occupational scale. And 40 per cent had been employed in the same job for 3 to 20 years. At the age of about 40 some 80 per cent were married, and the great majority of their children were said to be progressing normally at school. In one small group of adults whose intelligence was tested, the mean had risen from an original Stanford-Binet I.Q. of 58 to a Wechsler-Bellevue I.Q. of 81 (this, however, is difficult to interpret on account of regression effects and differences between the two scales).

Another investigation which aroused widespread controversy was that of Schmidt (1946) in Chicago. She studied 252 children, aged 12–14 who had been classified as feebleminded, and who attended a school for 3 years whose curriculum was specially designed to increase emotional and social adjustment, as well as to improve academic and manipulative skills. Subsequently they were followed up for $1\frac{1}{2}$ to $4\frac{1}{2}$ years. Over the $7\frac{1}{2}$-year period the mean Stanford-Binet I.Q. rose from 52 to 89, whereas a control group who attended ordinary special schools dropped from I.Q. 60 to 56. Many of them returned to high school, and 27 per cent completed a 4-year course. When last followed up, 83 per cent were in employment, two-thirds in clerical or moderately skilled work. By contrast the controls showed very poor educational and employment records. Equally striking improvements are quoted in tests of emotional stability.

Some psychologists frankly question the authenticity of the whole investigation, and admittedly it is difficult to evaluate the significance of Schmidt's test results. But her findings on occupational adjustment are not dissimilar to those of Charles. Thus it would appear that, by providing the right kind of educational environment and paying attention to emotional adjustment, a large proportion of children once diagnosed as defectives can grow up into reasonably capable adults. On the other hand, we also know that those who are institutionalised, or who attend the ordinary special school, tend to remain at almost the same level or even to decline in ability.

In this country, Mundy (1957), working with imbecile women, found that patients who were put into jobs and allowed to live outside an institution gained in two years some 6 to 12 I.Q. points over control cases who remained institutionalised. However, it may well have been that the experimental group possessed more initiative and were better adjusted than the controls, so that they would be more likely to improve in any case. Clarke (1958) has published several studies of feebleminded youths and young adults, which indicate that bad home conditions in early life play some part in retarding their development. In the first of these, patients were tested with Wechsler-Bellevue on entry to an institution and again after 2 years. Among those who (unknown to the tester) came from a reasonably good background, there was an increase of 4·1 I.Q. points, which was just the same as the normal practice effect. But among those who came from bad homes, where there had been gross neglect or rejection, the increase averaged 9·7 points; thus the 5·6 points difference could reasonably be attributed to the improved conditions. Further retests led to further, smaller, rises; but the provision of special vocational training did not appear to make more than another 2 to 3 points difference.

Note that the range of increases reported by British investigators is far smaller than that claimed by Wellman and Schmidt, though the former were, of course, dealing with older and lower-grade subjects, and followed them only over a few years. At least their evidence is sufficient to negate any complacent acceptance of the I.Q. as unchangeable. But it would be equally false to rush to the opposite extreme, since we certainly do not have any recipe for converting persons of defective intelligence into normals.

EFFECTS OF SECONDARY SCHOOLING AND ADULT EMPLOYMENT

There is much stronger evidence for the influence of secondary and later education on the I.Q. than of nursery or primary. As pointed out in Chapter One, average adult test scores are no higher than those of 13–16 year olds. Yet at the same time many studies have shown that high school and college students continue to increase their scores from 15 up to 20 years and over. Indeed, Dearborn and Rothney (1941), on the basis of repeated testing of children in their 'teens, predict that the final maximum is not reached until 30. The only plausible way of reconciling these findings is to allow that growth continues so long as education or

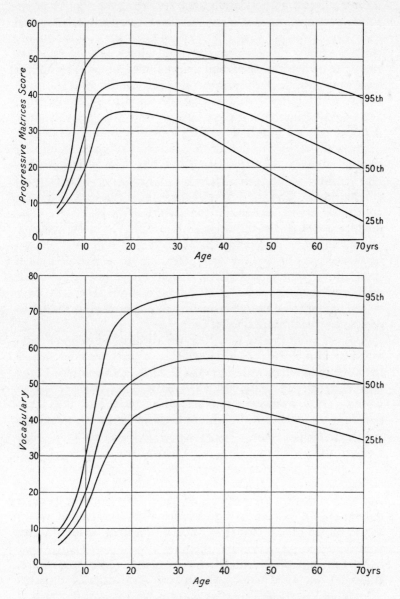

FIG. 7 Age changes in scores on Progressive Matrices and Vocabulary
Tests at the 95th, 50th and 25th Percentiles.

other intellectually stimulating conditions continue, though probably never beyond about 25–30 years, and that when such stimulation ceases a decline sets in. The majority of the population, including almost all average and dull adolescents, finish their education around 14 or 16, and tend to enter jobs and indulge in leisure pursuits which do little to 'exercise' their 'brains'. The more privileged minority continue their education to 18, 22 or later, and mostly enter jobs and pursue interests which make more demands on their minds. Thus their increase presumably roughly balances the majority's decline, producing a fairly steady average level in the total population from 15 to 25. This is illustrated in Fig. 7, which shows the characteristic 'fanning out' of test norms among adults. The more intelligent individuals tend to go on increasing longer and decline more slowly, whereas the least intelligent stop earlier and decline more rapidly. Similar evidence was obtained by classifying the Matrices scores of some 90,000 naval recruits during the war according to age and civilian occupation (Vernon and Parry, 1949). The more 'intellectual' categories such as clerks, electrical or woodworkers not only scored higher at all ages than mates and labourers, but started to decline later and more slowly.

A direct indication of the effects of advanced education is provided by Lorge's (1945) and Husén's (1951) investigations, where the same individuals were tested as children and as adults. Lorge reckoned that, at 34, adults who had received university education were 2 M.A. years superior to others who possessed the same intelligence at 14 but had had no further schooling. Husén tested 722 men entering the Army at 20 whose I.Q.s at 10 years were known, and found that those who had matriculated had gained 12 I.Q. points relative to those who had had no secondary education.

That the quality rather than the length of schooling makes a difference is indicated by a research (Vernon, 1957a) in which almost all the boys in the 14 secondary schools of an English city were tested at 14 years, and their results compared with their I.Q.s at the time of secondary school selection 3 to 4 years earlier. Allowing for initial differences between boys entering different schools, and for regression effects, there were now differences of up to 12 points between boys in the 'best' and 'worst' schools. The combined grammar and technical school boys had apparently gained 7 points over the combined modern schools.[1] Much of this difference might well be due to the grammar school boys coming from better homes, with more favourable attitudes to education; but this would none the less be an environmental effect. The results supply strong grounds for suspecting that some secondary modern and all-age schools, actually inhibit the full growth of intelligence over the 11- to 15-year period: if the pupils and staff are bored or resentful and the teaching mechanical; whereas other modern schools, together with most technical and grammar schools, are relatively successful in stimulating the mind and bringing out potentialities more fully. According to a further research by Lovell (1955), it is mental flexibility in particular, and the capacity for forming new concepts, which are affected by the adolescent's intellectual and emotional circumstances, that is those very capacities which are most subject to deterioration in adulthood (cf. p. 86).

An objection may well be raised to these conclusions, namely that they run counter to psychological teaching about transfer of training. Has it not been proved that mental faculties like reasoning and memory cannot be trained in general, and is not this notion of 'exercising' or 'stimulating' the mind suspiciously close to the discarded notion of formal discipline? This is true. But it should be remembered that the alterations in intelligence described above are rather small, and quite difficult to demonstrate except by surveys of large numbers of pupils or adults. Moreover, psychologists realise now that the initial reaction against transfer of training went too far; a majority of experiments have actually demonstrated a good deal of transfer under appropriate conditions. Again, the most relevant experiments—those of Thorndike and his collaborators (Brolyer, 1927)—although they are usually quoted as disproving any 'formal disciplinary' effect, in fact gave some positive support. Thorndike compared the intelligence test changes among high school pupils who took a variety of school

---

[1] This finding is disputed by Pidgeon and Yates (1957); however, if their figures are adjusted for expected regression effects they accord closely with Vernon's. It is interesting to speculate whether the strong positive skew in Terman-Merrill I.Q.s at 11 years (cf. ftn. p. 55) may not be due to the success of junior schools in stimulating the intelligence of above-average pupils who have a chance of success in the selection (or Scottish qualifying) examinations. It appears to be considerably more marked than in America.

subjects during a year's ordinary schooling. The differences were very small, but on the whole the biggest relative improvement occurred among those who had taken arithmetic, maths, physics and chemistry; Latin, French and social studies gave more inconsistent, though predominantly positive, results; whereas there was a relative decrease among those taking dramatic art, cooking, sewing, stenography, biology and agriculture. Unfortunately the investigation did not include adolescents who had no secondary schooling at all over the period, but we can be fairly certain that they would have shown less improvement still or a decline.

DISCUSSION

Many psychologists, while accepting the experimental findings we have outlined in this chapter and in our account of race differences (p. 174), would assert that they show environmental effects upon intelligence test performance rather than changes in intelligence itself. This is a difficult point, particularly since we have agreed that coaching or practice at tests does improve facility at such tests without necessarily improving underlying intelligence. But we would suggest that disagreements among psychologists are largely verbal in nature. R. B. Cattell and others, who stress heredity, prefer to keep the term 'intelligence' for Hebb's Intelligence A (cf. p. 34), whereas we regard this innate potentiality as of theoretical interest (although its existence is clearly demonstrated by some of the evidence cited), and apply 'intelligence' to the developed ability which can be observed and measured. Maybe it would save confusion if the word was abandoned as being liable to mislead teachers and the public; and we have seen that there is a move in this direction.

We should realise, however, that when the layman talks of a child as being intelligent and thinks he is referring to 'native wit', he is really describing Intelligence B—that is, much the same product of heredity and environment as the tests measure. The child brought up in a very unfavourable environment does not merely obtain a poorer I.Q. than he might otherwise have done on Terman-Merrill. He is genuinely poorer at school learning, in the level of employment for which he is fitted, and in other behaviour of an intellectual character. By contrast, the child who has been coached on group tests is superior only in that rather specific type of behaviour, and we have no evidence that his school work or other intelligent activities benefit.

Incidentally, this brings out the fallacy in some left-wing criticisms of intelligence tests—that they reflect social-class differences. The average middle-class child admittedly has an advantage at such tests, partly because of his upbringing and partly, as we have seen, because of superior inheritance. But this impurity in the tests, or failure to measure truly innate intelligence, is quite irrelevant from the pragmatic standpoint. What really matters is that, on the average, he is capable of more advanced school work; and that when, for example, he enters the Services, he tends to be quicker at learning and more capable at any skilled job. This was proved time and again during World War II. The same is true of the working-class child whose intelligence test scores and educational achievements are superior, despite an unfavourable background.

It is in this sense, then, that intelligence is a product of both heredity and environment during the early years of childhood, and is susceptible to stunting or to further development during adolescence and early adulthood. In this sense, also, its proper growth may be inhibited by emotional maladjustment, so that big increases in I.Q. (paralleled by improvements at school and elsewhere) are often reported as a result of child guidance treatment,[1] or of the treatment mentioned by Schmidt and Clarke. This is no revolutionary doctrine; for geneticists do not regard the genes as solely responsible even for our innate physical attributes. They would hold rather that the genes provide the potentiality for any attribute to develop under suitable environmental conditions.

There may still be some conflict regarding the relative weight of hereditary and environmental contributions. This book has stressed the importance of upbringing, social differences and education, whereas the careful statistical analyses of Burt and others appear to demonstrate the overwhelming importance of heredity. Such studies, however, have generally been carried out on children who were fairly homogeneous, and for whom environmental stimulation did not vary very widely. Many of the separated identical twins were brought up in quite similar homes; possibly some were not even separated until some time after

---

[1] Admittedly, it is sometimes difficult to distinguish such increases from those due merely to the child's lack of co-operation when he first comes to the clinic.

birth. Within any one culture, such as our own and the American, the apparent effects of environment are reduced, since all children tend to hear and learn much the same language, and to come in contact with the same pictorial or other symbols. Thus they all have the opportunity for acquiring much the same simple concepts of space, time, number, etc., from 0 to 4 years, and from 5 onwards they receive a more or less standardised education, which also trains them to attend to oral or printed questions and to answer them quickly. Such influences do, of course, vary appreciably between different social classes and different families, or even between children within any one family, though apparently not enough to raise the environmental component of the I.Q. to more than 20 to 25 per cent. The simpler concepts which the preschool child is building up are probably provided for almost as well in a poor, overcrowded, as in a rich, cultured home. Emotional influences perhaps have a greater effect than intellectual ones at this age. Thus there is some evidence that intelligence develops better in a 'democratic' home atmosphere than when the parents are either too autocratic or rejecting, or too indulgent and over-protective (cf. Baldwin, 1945).

With children generally, then, heredity combined with environmental factors common to all has something like a 75 per cent influence. But the heterogeneity of environment begins to increase when children are segregated into different types of secondary schools and after they leave school. Hence its effects are much more noticeable in the 'teens, when children are at the stage of acquiring the more complex concepts and modes of thinking. From 15 to 20, indeed, educational stimulation differs so widely from one person to another that it becomes the major determinant of further growth in intelligence. And when we go outside a single culture, the variations in concepts, habits of thought and in attitudes to intellectual tasks are so wide that useful comparisons can no longer be made by any intelligence tests.

The same stricture is true, even if to a lesser extent, of comparisons between sub-groups within a culture, such as different social classes. But much depends on our purpose in applying intelligence tests. When we give them for diagnosing probable scholastic and vocational capacities, then the environmental influence on test scores is actually an advantage; it produces better predictions. But we are not entitled to apply tests for studying genetic differences, except in those rare circumstances such as Lawrence's experiment (p. 144), where the environmental variations have been controlled. The difficulties of this control are well illustrated in our next section.

FAMILY SIZE AND THE DECLINE IN NATIONAL INTELLIGENCE

It has been shown by the work of Burt (1946), Thomson, Fraser Roberts, Cattell and others that children from large families tend to have lower intelligence than those from small ones. In the present writer's survey of Army recruits (Vernon, 1951), for example, the average I.Q. of those who were only children, or who had but one sibling, was about 106; but with each additional sibling the figure declined till those from families of 13 and over averaged only 87. Indeed, a negative correlation of —0·2 to —0·3 is regularly found in most western European countries and North America, though the trend is sometimes reversed among the more intelligent, middle- and upper-class parents, depending partly on the family allowances granted by the State, partly on the current attitudes towards birth control and to having children. Note that this differential birth-rate is not merely a matter of social class. Labourers do tend to have larger families than skilled workers, and skilled workers than professional people; but within any one class, such as skilled workers, the small-family children obtain higher I.Q.s than large-family ones. Naturally a correlation of around 0·3 permits of great variations. There are still some large families of very intelligent children, and some dull only children. However, the trend causes serious concern to population experts and eugenists, since it would appear that the brightest stocks are generally failing to reproduce themselves and are being progressively swamped by the less bright. Probably this has been going on for a very long time, but it has become more marked in the twentieth century because the differential death-rate (which used to wipe out more lower than upper-class children) has been reduced by advances in public health, and because scientific family regulation has become much more common, particularly among middle- and upper-class parents. Fraser Roberts has found that the latter tend to start having children later in life, to space them out more and to stop sooner than duller families (1939).

It is quite easy to calculate from the test scores of the present generation the probable distribution of intelligence in the next generation, and Table IX shows a cautious estimate made by Burt from 1920 figures up to the year 2000. The decline of about

TABLE IX

I.Q.s DISTRIBUTIONS OBTAINED IN 1920 AND
PREDICTED AT LATER DATES ON THE BASIS OF
FAMILY SIZE

Intelligence Level	I.Q.	Proportion in 1920	No. of Children per Family	Proportions expected in: 1950	Proportions expected in: 2000
Superior (scholarship, etc.) . . .	130+	1·8	2·3	1·4	0·8
Good . . .	115–29	12·2	2·7	10·3	7·6
Average + . .	100–14	35·1	3·3	33·4	29·9
Average − . .	85–99	37·5	3·6	38·6	40·5
Dull and backward .	70–84	11·9	4·2	14·2	17·9
Very dull (feeble-minded, etc.) .	Below 70	1·5	4·7	2·1	3·3
Average I.Q. .		100·0		98·5	96·0

1½ points in the average I.Q. per generation is bad enough; but even more striking are the predicted effects at the top and bottom ends. The numbers of children with I.Q. 130+ are expected to be halved in 80 years, and of those below 70 to be roughly doubled.

Some supporting evidence was provided by the Royal Commissions on mental deficiency in 1907 and 1929, which claimed to discover a big increase in the numbers of defectives in the population between these dates. However, the figures have been widely disputed, because of the difficulties of ensuring complete ascertainment. Hence the Scottish Council for Research in Education (1949) undertook to apply the same test to all Scottish 11 year olds in 1947 as had been used 15 years earlier. The gap of about half a generation was, of course, rather short, but with such large numbers a decline of even half a point should be noticeable. Actually, as explained in the previous chapter, there was a rise in the mean group test score, probably attributable to greater test-sophistication of many of the second group. But representative samples of 7-800 had also been given Stanford-Binet and/or Terman-Merrill—that is, individual tests which were unlikely to be more familiar in 1947; and from their results it was calculated that there had been no change either up or down. Despite the most careful analysis of the data, it has not been possible to decide why the predictions of a decline were falsified. Some geneticists consider that nature provides a kind of biological stabilising or compensating mechanism.[1] Alternatively, improvements in child health and education over the period might sufficiently raise the average I.Q. to mask a small genetic decline. But if the low intelligence of large-family children were merely an environmental phenomenon, then of course no decline at all would be expected. It might well be argued that family circumstances and the amount of attention and stimulation given to each child are impaired when the number of children rises above two. If this were the complete explanation, the later children should perhaps be less intelligent than the earlier. There is, in fact, a slight tendency for the first and last child in any family of three or more to be more intelligent than the middle ones, and these are the ones who often get most parental attention. But there is no further correlation between I.Q. and position in family. Thus the only safe conclusion is that we do not know. There may be some genuine, though small, tendency for the genetically less-intelligent stocks to be more fertile which will need to be watched. But so far this has had no demonstrable effect on Intelligence B.

[1] Thus L. S. Penrose points out that dull parents do not only have dull children. They have some very dull ones who are likely to be infertile, and some relatively bright or near-to-average ones who are fertile. Thus the mean intelligence of their descendants is somewhat higher than would be expected on the basis of regression, and this may balance out the decline attributable to their large numbers. Certainly something of the kind would seem to operate in the case of height and other physical qualities, which are very largely genetically determined, and are likewise negatively correlated with fertility. For we can be certain that any marked decline in the average height of the population over the past 50 years or so would have been detected.

Chapter Ten

SOME RESULTS OF MENTAL TESTING

DISTRIBUTIONS OF INTELLIGENCE AND ATTAINMENTS

THE conventional I.Q. categories and their approximate proportions in the total population are shown in Table X. These are

TABLE X

THE DISTRIBUTION OF INTELLIGENCE

I.Q.	Category		Per cent
130 & over	Very superior		2½
120–9	Superior		6½
110–19	Above Average or Bright Normal . . .		16
90–109	Average		50
80–89	Below Average or Dull Normal . . .		16
70–79	Dull		6½
40–69	Highgrade Feebleminded or Moron	Mental	
20–39	Lowgrade Defective—Imbecile	Defective .	2½
0–19	„ „ —Idiot		

based on the assumption of a normal distribution, with a Standard Deviation of 15—an assumption which, as we have seen, is seldom exactly fulfilled. The categories should not be taken too literally. For example, there is scarcely anything to choose between 109 (average) and 110 (above average); an individual can easily alter one category up or down on retesting. In particular, a very low I.Q. does not necessarily show mental defect or feeblemindedness.

Categories of attainment in reading, arithmetic and other subjects are not so well established. But generally, Educational Quotients of 115 upwards (16 per cent) would be considered Superior, and 85 (16 per cent) or 80 (9 per cent) downwards as Backward. A large-scale survey of reading comprehension ability among school-leavers and adults, carried out by the Ministry of Education (1950), attempted to fix acceptable, even if arbitrary, borderlines for literacy in terms of Reading Ages. Our Table

TABLE XI

DISTRIBUTIONS OF READING ABILITY AMONG
15-YEAR-OLDS

Grade of Reading	Reading Age	All 15-Year	Grammar-Technical	Modern Schools	Post-war Norms
Superior .	17:0+	8·5	29·6	1·5	14·7
Average + .	13:8+	38·0	57·5	25·3	37·0[1]
Average − .	12:0+	25·5	10·9	33·5	31·9
Backward .	9:0+	21·8	2·0	32·9	14·3
Semi-literate .	7:0+	4·6	0·0	5·6	} 2·1
Illiterate .	Under 7:0	1·6	0·0	1·2	

shows the proportions found in 1949 for all 15-year-olds, and for selective (grammar and technical) schools and non-selective (modern and unreorganised) schools. These figures are based on pre-war norms, and the last column shows the proportions according to post-war norms; here, of course, the percentages of Superior and Backward or worse approximate closely to the expected 16 per cent.[1] Note the strong differentiation between the different types of school. Some 40 per cent of all secondary modern school-leavers were backward or worse by pre-war standards, though the number of complete illiterates was much smaller than is sometimes feared. Later surveys (Ministry of Education, 1957) with the same test showed that the proportion of Backward or worse was reduced by about 5 per cent over the next 8 years, although pre-war standards had still not been fully regained.

Until some agreement is reached on definite categories of attainment in other subjects, there is little point in trying to describe how they are distributed in the population at large. However, some indication of standards among school-leavers and young adults is given by the following list of spelling words and arithmetic sums. These fall approximately at the 95th, 85th, . . . 5th percentile levels; that is, the first word or sum would be roughly characteristic of the attainments of the best 10 per cent of the population, the last one of the weakest 10 per cent.

[1] The dividing-line between Average+ and Average− was taken as 14:6 years for post-war leavers because of the change in age of leaving.

Percentile Level	Spelling	Arithmetic and Mathematics
95th	PARALLEL	$\sqrt{12^2 + 5^2} =$
85th	ACQUIRED	What is simple interest on £250 for 2 years at 5 per cent?
75th	DISEASE	What is the area in square yards of a 30 ft. by 24 ft. room?
65th	SCARCELY	If $3x + 2 = 14$, $x =$
55th	CONCEALED	Write one-quarter as a decimal
45th	SCHOLAR	Simplify $\dfrac{45}{26} \div \dfrac{9}{52}$
35th	PRESSURE	$\frac{3}{4} + \frac{1}{2} =$
25th	JUICE	How many pints in a gallon and a half?
15th	DOZEN	Subtract: s. d. 8 6 −4 8
5th	TABLE	Add: 536 +715

There are, it should be noted, considerable sex differences, females being relatively superior in spelling and inferior in arithmetic. Moreover, the standards of 14–15 year olds tend to be somewhat higher than those of young adults. For there is strong evidence that the attainments of school-leavers in these drilled subjects is maintained or improved only among the more able who continue their schooling, or who enter jobs where they continue to practice their skills (cf. Norris, 1940). The average pupil tends to decline appreciably by 18, and the more backward ones more rapidly. Indeed, the lowest 10 per cent of pupils who approximated (at best) to 11-year level in arithmetic and spelling before leaving, have dropped back to 8-year level some 4 years later. Reading comprehension, by contrast, seems to go on improving, since the great majority do continue some sort of reading in daily life.

A short digression is appropriate here on the alleged decline in educational standards over the past 50 years, which is often bewailed by public speakers and writers to the Press. We suspect that, apart from the war-time decline previously mentioned (p. 116), these judgments are based almost wholly on comparisons between unrepresentative samples. For example, there are more than twice as many grammar schools as there were 50 years ago and, despite more efficient selection nowadays (by ability rather than by income), this inevitably means that somewhat lower ability strata are admitted. The best grammar school pupils are probably no worse, but they are more diluted. Equally, present-day modern and unreorganised schools are more effectively creamed, so that their average standard must be lower too, unless the efficiency of their education has much improved.[1] An equally striking redistribution of employment has occurred between about 1910 and 1950. The numbers engaged in Textiles, Clothing, Mining, Agriculture and Fishing have dropped from $29\frac{1}{2}$ per cent to $18\frac{1}{2}$ per cent; but the numbers in Metal and Chemical Manufacturing and Engineering, in Administrative and Professional Services have risen from $20\frac{1}{2}$ per cent to $37\frac{1}{2}$ per cent. Such favoured occupations as electrical and other skilled engineering, the Civil Service and Local Government are probably attracting so much more of the available talent that other employers have to go much farther down the scale than they used. Thus business men's secretaries may seem 'illiterate' nowadays, but not because there has been any decline in the amount of intelligence or education in the population as a whole. The critics who deplore declines in cultural interests are also probably not comparing like with like. They are usually people of good intelligence and education who base their standards on a circle of acquaintances similar to themselves, and are shocked by the leisure pursuits, or the favourite newspapers and broadcasts of the mass of the present-day population. A fairer comparison would be between the present poorly cultured majority and the slum-dweller of 40 years ago, who worked much longer hours and whose favourite leisure pursuit was alcohol. Actually, there is ample evidence of far more library reading, more adult education classes, more amateur musical and dramatic societies now than in the past.

---

[1] It may sound puzzling that average levels in both types of school can fall without a drop in the total population. These hypothetical figures illustrate it.

Grammar school 14 per cent with mean E.Q. 125 + Modern school 86 per cent with mean E.Q. 96 give an overall average E.Q. 100.

Grammar school 28 per cent with mean E.Q. 121 + Modern school 72 per cent with mean E.Q. 92 also gives an average of 100.

CHARACTERISTICS OF THE TAILS OF THE DISTRIBUTION: MENTAL DEFECTIVES

Mental deficiency is a legal rather than a psychological term. It refers to adults who "require care, supervision and control for their own protection or for the protection of others", that is roughly the ½ per cent most incapable of the population. Certifiable children were defined as those "incapable of receiving proper benefit from the instruction in ordinary schools", that is about 2½ per cent. However, with the passing of the 1944 Education Act, the term was restricted to relatively low-grade children or those presenting serious behaviour problems; while the lowest 10 per cent or so of the school population in attainments (those with E.Q.s below 80, regardless of I.Q.) are classed as Educationally Subnormal or E.S.N. Because of insufficient provision, only a small proportion of the most backward are, in fact, transferred to special schools or classes. Likewise, the number of available places in institutions and hospitals largely determines how many defectives are certified.

While certification (in the case of children, called 'ascertainment') is rightly based on social and educational criteria, and is done by a doctor, it is usual to have them tested, preferably by a qualified psychologist, with the Terman-Merrill or Wechsler scales if only because these provide a more objective criterion of intellectual subnormality than do judgments of adjustment. Nevertheless, there are many certified adults and children with I.Q.s of 80 and over who are too emotionally unstable to be allowed to go at large, and many with I.Q.s of 60 or under who are sufficiently stable to get along fairly well in school or in employment. On the whole, however, low intelligence and poor adjustment tend to go together; defectives are also poorer in health and physique than normals. Clarke (1958) brings out the tremendous variation in types and causes of mental deficiency. The lower-grade imbeciles and idiots, as we have seen, arise largely from pathological causes and/or rare genes, whereas the higher-grade feebleminded are often referred to as 'sub-cultural'. Some of the latter may show pathological symptoms, and probably most of them are low in Intelligence A, but generally also they are victims of their environment. The lower grades never progress much beyond the level of development of young children, and have to be cared for at home or in institutions; many cannot learn to speak or to keep themselves clean, though others can sometimes be taught simple routine activities, or housework or gardening.

With high-grade morons and the top of the imbecile group, however, it would be rash to set any such limit (cf. Wallin, 1956; Sarason and Gladwin, 1958; Clarke, 1958). It used to be said that they were educable roughly up to their maximum Mental Age; for example, a 15-year old with I.Q. 60 should be able to read as well as an average 9-year old. And it was believed that they could succeed only in unskilled employment under sheltered conditions. Many, in fact, never make appreciable educational progress, either through poor adjustment, continued adverse home circumstances, or through vegetating in special schools or institutions. But others are more successful (even if Schmidt's claims are greatly exaggerated); and they can often be trained in fairly skilled work, though taking a good deal longer to learn than normals. Indeed, their practical capacities are likely to be superior to their verbal ones (cf. p. 118). (The occurrence of *idiots savants* who combine exceptional numerical or other talents with very low intelligence is extremely rare.) They need more guidance and supervision than average persons, but they respond normally to incentives and to a helpful environment.

It has often been thought that defective children and adults are particularly apt to become delinquents and criminals, presumably on the grounds that crime is an unintelligent way of gaining one's ends. But it is quite untrue that even a majority of prisoners and delinquents are of very low intelligence; many score well above average. Indeed, some investigators have obtained distributions very similar to those in the non-criminal population, though the majority would place their mean I.Q. round about 85 to 90, i.e. in the backward class. The interpretation even of this degree of subnormality is dubious. After all, unintelligent delinquents are more likely to be caught than intelligent ones. Moreover, we tend to find both more crime and more persons of low intelligence in overcrowded, slum conditions and in the lower socio-economic grades. Thus the association may be as spurious as that which doubtless exists between criminality and—say—a liking for fish and chips. The sensible conclusion would seem to be that of Burt, in his *Young Delinquent* (1925a), that low intelligence may be one factor in delinquency, though usually combined with tempera-

mental, environmental and other factors. Apart from these handicaps the defective child, according to Wallin, is more likely to be
happy-go-lucky and tractable than criminal.

GENIUS AND THE HIGHLY INTELLIGENT

A mine of information on the characteristics of the top end of
the distribution is provided by Terman's *Genetic Studies of Genius*
(1925-47). Vol. II selects some three hundred persons of acknowledged eminence from history and, by a careful analysis of
their biographies as children and their recorded achievements at
various ages, tries to estimate their childhood I.Q.s. A few, such as
John Stuart Mill, Grotius and Leibnitz, were clearly capable at the
age of, say, 6 of intellectual operations that would tax a normal
12-year old; and their brilliance persisted. Thus it is reasonable to
credit them with I.Q.s approaching 200. The average for the
whole group was 155; that is, very superior. But this means that
some were distinctly lower. Oliver Cromwell, for example, was
estimated at 110 only. However, the proportion showing little
promise in childhood was far smaller than many laymen imagine.
Another common misbelief is that genius tends to be narrowly
confined to special fields. Actually, versatility was the rule rather
than the exception. Apart perhaps from musicians and artists,
those who were outstanding in one special field were generally
above average in several other fields. Thus *g*-factor theory still
has some application even at this level. But Terman freely admits
that traits of personality are at least as important as intelligence in
the formation of genius, and points out, too, how often historical
accident and favourable environment play a part.

The other volumes start, as it were, at the other end and study
the characteristics of some 1,500 children with I.Q.s of 135 upwards, representing the brightest 1 per cent of the Californian
10-16 year population. These have now been followed over 35
years, and though Terman does not claim that any are or will be
geniuses, they certainly show very remarkable achievements.
When originally compared with a large control group of normal
children they were far advanced educationally in all subjects, as
would be expected. Their average E.Q. was 140, though in terms
of school grades it was only 114 because the schools had failed to
realise their superiority. Less expected was their general superiority
in health and growth. Probably it is because the very bright child

is so often the youngest in his class and is being compared with much older average children that he is sometimes thought of as puny. Their range of interests was also wider and superior in quality. For instance, they read more and better books and made twice as many collections. So far as could be determined from tests and ratings, they tended also to be superior in social and emotional development and moral character. It did seem, however, as though the brightest of all, with I.Q.s 170+, tend rather more frequently to experience difficulties of adjustment at home or school unless brought up with other bright children.

Vol. IV, which traces the adult characteristics of 96 per cent of the original group, is particularly interesting. The occupational distribution for men, compared with that for the general population, is shown in Table XII. It will be seen that over two-thirds are

TABLE XII

OCCUPATIONAL DISTRIBUTION FOR TERMAN'S GIFTED GROUP (MALE)

Occupational Group	Gifted Per cent	General Population
Professional . . .	45·4	5·7
Semi-professional and higher business . . .	25·7	8·1
Clerical and skilled trades .	20·7	24·3
Farming	1·2	12·4
Semi-skilled . . .	6·2	31·6
Slightly skilled and labouring	0·7	17·8

in the two highest grades, but that at the same time there is a small proportion, 8 per cent, in the three lowest (cf. p. 123).[1] Similarly, over two-thirds of men and women had graduated from college, though 5 per cent also failed. Twice as many had obtained higher degrees as do graduates in general, and five to eight times as many had Ph.D.s. Yet the gifted group also showed a superior record of extra-curricular activities—they were not merely bookish. There was no evidence that educational acceleration (i.e. going up to college at an early age) had been in any way harmful. Again,

[1] In the ensuing 10 years there was a further rise. By 1955, 86·3 per cent were in the top two, and only 1·2 per cent in the bottom two, groups.

a larger proportion of men than in the general population had had war service, and nearly 75 per cent of these obtained commissions. The delinquency and crime rate of the gifted group was extremely low, and the incidence of mental breakdown was no greater than in the population at large. There was no indication that they tended to become 'cranks'; thus their political affiliations were similar to those of the general population. Their marriage rate was higher than that of average graduates, and their divorce rate normal. Their fertility so far was low, but their children— many of whom have been tested—had a high mean I.Q. of 128. This figure is, of course, lower than that of the gifted parents, as would be expected both because the spouse was usually less intelligent and because of regression. Seven per cent of the children fell below 100, but 15 per cent (as compared with about 1 per cent in the general population) scored in the same high category as the parent.

Much additional case-study material is given on the achievements, publications, etc., of individual members of the group. Special attention is also paid to those who careers were relatively unsuccessful. Their initial ability and school records were no whit inferior, though they were clearly beginning to drop behind in college. Their environments tended to be less favourable, and in most instances certain weaknesses of character and emotional adjustment had begun to show themselves in childhood. Nevertheless, Terman's researches certainly demonstrate that a high I.Q. in childhood is strongly predictive of superior educational achievement and a very favourable factor in the vocational and other spheres. The child of exceptionally low intelligence shows much the same characteristics in reverse.

SEX DIFFERENCES

Numerous comparisons have shown the average scores of boys and girls, or men and women, to be the same on general intelligence tests, though there are some differences on the group factors that enter into many tests. Girls do a little better on most verbal tests and on tests involving rote memory, boys on tests of inductive reasoning and arithmetical ability.[1] But there is a great deal

[1] From about 1940 to 1950 girls usually did better than boys at the intelligence and arithmetic group tests in 11-year selection examinations, as well as in English, and different borderlines often had to be drawn for entry to grammar

of overlapping, and the average differences seldom exceed about 4 points of I.Q. The most marked difference occurs on spatial and mechanical tests. Whether there is any innate factor in boys' superiority, we do not know. It might well be attributed to the cultural influences in our own civilisation which encourage boys to develop physical, constructional and mechanical interests.

Many surveys of intelligence and attainments have also demonstrated that the range or spread of ability (as distinct from the average performance) is slightly more restricted in girls. The evidence is not unanimous, but there do seem to be larger proportions of very able and of very backward boys. Society also recognises more men than women of outstanding talent in almost every walk of life, and there are more male mental defectives. Obviously it would be rash to argue that innate factors are responsible, since our culture supplies far less encouragement and opportunity to women. Moreover, female defectives are less troublesome to look after at home, so that this difference might be merely one of ascertainment. Again, any difference may be not so much one of ability as of temperamental traits and interests, innate and acquired. The boy, in our Western culture at least, tends to be more rebellious and more ambitious than the girl, and may thus either fall further behind or progress further ahead in school work and in intellectual activities generally.

AGE CHANGES

One of the remarkable findings of American Army testing in 1917–18 was that adult recruits scored no higher than 13-year children. Other tests, too, have shown little or no increase beyond 15, and it was widely accepted that intellectual growth reaches its maximum at about this age and then stops. Both information, occupational skills and worldly experience obviously go on increasing much later, but these were distinguished from intelligence—the capacity for problem solving, for seeing relations and for new learning, which not only failed to improve but soon started to decline. On tests of a more informational type like Vocabulary there seem to be rises up to the 30s, and relatively

schools. It seems likely that boys were more seriously affected by war-time relaxations of home discipline and upsets to schooling. By the later 1950s, boys had generally caught up in intelligence tests and regained their superiority in arithmetic (cf. Emmett, 1954).

slow decay. But on abstraction and non-verbal reasoning (such as Progressive Matrices) the decline begins in the 20s, or even earlier (cf. Vernon and Parry, 1949). Fig. 7 is adapted from Raven's standardisation of his Vocabulary and Matrices tests over the age range 5 to 65 years (Foulds and Raven, 1948). By 60, the average adult has dropped back to the same level as 10-year children on Matrices.[1] Similarly, in the Wechsler-Bellevue scale, scores on Information, Comprehension and Vocabulary sink only slightly with age; Block Design, Similarities, Substitution and Digit Memory decline much more rapidly. Wechsler supplies an index of mental deterioration, based on contrasting tests which do and which do not hold up in this way. It is generally found also that older persons are particularly handicapped in speeded tests; hence it is usual to allow more ample time limits in group tests for adults than for children.

However, these results, based on comparisons between different-aged cross-sections of the population, must be accepted with considerable caution. We have already seen that adult scores on intelligence tests may be markedly affected by the education they have received. Thus much of the apparent decline from 20 to 60 may be due to the fact that present-day 60-year olds were less well educated forty to fifty years ago than are present-day 20-year olds. Hence several longitudinal studies, where the same individuals were retested after 20 or more years, have shown little decline, or even increases (cf. Nisbet, 1957), though these, too, have their snags. The individuals would not remember the actual test items, but they might be more test-sophisticated or better motivated; usually, also, they have been above average in initial level and therefore—as Fig. 7 shows—less apt to decline in any case.

Particularly illuminating is the work of Welford (1958) and the Cambridge Psychology Department on ageing. Using a variety of tests of the acquisition of skilled movements, they showed that older workers are usually able to compensate for such obvious handicaps as decreased visual and auditory acuity, speed of movement and reaction time. Because of their greater experience they are often as good, or better, at familiar tasks, especially those involving accuracy and responsibility which can be done at their

---

[1] Raven's more recent data suggest a steeper decline in Vocabulary after age 60 than is shown in the Figure, though it is extremely difficult to ensure that samples of 'normal' older persons are really representative.

own rate. They are less good when they have to work under stress of speed, and are generally slower and less mentally alert. But they chiefly show their age in comprehending, interpreting and organising new material—whether it be the perceptual and motor elements in a skilled job or the verbal data in a logical or intelligence test problem. Indeed, their previous habitual modes of response often make them unduly inflexible and less capable of adapting to these new requirements. Similarly, the work of Thorndike (1928) and others shows that adults of, say, 40 to 50 are little inferior to 15–20-year olds in the learning of straightforward topics like a new foreign language, but are much poorer at tasks which involve the breaking down of old habits, as in foreign language pronunciation.

Clearly it is too superficial to think of intelligence as a single entity growing to a maximum and declining. Rather there are qualitative changes with age, and our conventional intelligence tests hardly give scope to the ways in which the older person expresses his ability, though they rightly show that he is handicapped in rapid adaptation to, and solution of, new mental or physical problems. In other respects which we call wisdom, experience, judgment, knowledge and skill, he is a more capable member of the community until such time as his deteriorating sensory and motor capacities and increasing mental rigidity begin to outweigh these assets.

GEOGRAPHICAL DIFFERENCES

No one has tested sufficiently representative samples of the total U.K. population to say precisely which are the most or least intelligent regions. Nevertheless, both Moray House results at 11 (Emmett, 1954), and the writer's analysis of Army National Service tests (Vernon, 1951) show distinct differences between counties, ranging up to 6 or even 10 points of I.Q., though these two enquiries largely disagree in their findings. A few generalisations are possible.

  1. Much the most intelligent areas are those on the outskirts of large cities, for example the Home Counties around London; and the lowest are the overcrowded areas within such cities. This naturally follows from the distribution of intelligence among occupational classes.

  2. Areas with large Irish populations (e.g. Glasgow and Liver-

pool) and Welsh counties tend to score below average. This is not merely due to language handicaps, since it is found also with non-verbal tests. It too reflects occupational differences.

3. Urban children in all areas average some 2 points higher than rural, though this varies considerably from county to county, and has not been confirmed among adults. Numerous factors are involved here, and we would merely be airing our prejudices if we tried to assess the relative importance of the following:

(a) Brighter families may be more apt to migrate to the towns.

(b) The tests may favour the town child, both in their content or in the knowledge they assume and in their emphasis on quickness of thinking.

(c) Town children may be more sophisticated at taking tests, and better stimulated by the education received in the large urban schools.

RACIAL AND NATIONAL DIFFERENCES

A similar situation is found when we compare test results in different parts of the world, namely, there are quite large average differences (with much overlapping) but also grave doubts regarding their proper interpretation. The most extensive data are those from American Army tests of 1917–18, when hundreds of thousands of recruits were foreign born or the children of immigrants. Classified by country of origin, the approximate order of ability was: English, Scottish, Dutch, Danish, German, Canadian, Swedish, Norwegian, Irish, Austrian, Belgian, Turkish, Greek, Russian, Italian, Polish, Negro. These results are particularly questionable since it is unlikely that the immigrants were fair samples of their nations. Thus the British were mostly descended from the original pioneer stocks, whereas the Irish, Poles and others came from poorer peasant families emigrating in the late nineteenth century. It would be easy to prove the Irish more intelligent than the English by drawing samples from the best suburbs of Dublin and the worst slums of London.

However, other more careful studies confirm the general trend. Jews often get the highest average (say, I.Q. 105). American whites and north-west Europeans are all much the same, southern and eastern Europeans together with English-speaking Chinese and Japanese somewhat lower (say, 90 to 95), then American negroes (about 85), and Australian aborigines and other relatively primitive peoples lower still. At the same time individual differences within racial or national groups are far larger than differences between groups. At least 10 per cent of negroes surpass the average American white, and 10 per cent of whites score lower than the average negro.

There is probably no reputable psychologist nowadays who would maintain that these results represent genuine innate racial differences. Several might state the exact opposite, pointing out that the superior groups are just those which provide the best economic and social conditions and the best education. But the majority would be more likely to say that we cannot really make valid comparisons at all, since no tests can be devised which are 'culturally neutral'—that is, equally fair to groups with very different upbringing.

In a famous investigation, Klineberg (1935) tested negroes who had lived various lengths of time in New York; that is, in an area where their education and economic opportunities approximate much more closely to those of whites than in other areas from which they had moved, such as the Southern States. Those with less than a year's residence obtained an average Stanford-Binet I.Q. of $81\frac{1}{2}$, those with 4 years or more $87\frac{1}{2}$. The rise was even more marked on a verbal group test, but not found at all on a Paper Formboard (spatial) test. While this shows the importance of cultural factors, the fact that the average did not rise any farther towards 100 might be taken to mean that they are not all-important. Many investigators have used performance tests in different parts of the world (e.g. Porteus with his Mazes). Though the national and racial differences tend to be less marked than with verbal tests, they do not disappear; thus they are not purely linguistic or educational. But this does not prove anything, for it is obvious that white children gain far more experience with pictures, in manipulating blocks, or in drawing—i.e. with the kinds of materials and operations involved in performance tests—than do the children of more so-called backward peoples. However, studies of pre-school children generally yield rather smaller differences, and the inferiority is most marked when older negro children or young adults are tested for powers of abstract reasoning (cf. Shuey, 1958). From such results, it seems quite probable that genetic differences between racial and ethnic groups do exist

—at least in some aspects of intellectual ability—though we have no satisfactory way of proving it.

Biesheuvel (1949), who has wide experience in the testing of Africans, points out the fallacies of assuming that, by using pictures of objects familiar to the people concerned or abstract diagrams and shapes, cultural influences can be eliminated. The whole conception of pictorial representation on paper is outside the experience of many African tribes, and they may fail to recognise such pictures though quite familiar with similar carvings on ivory or leather. Again, their concepts of space and direction probably differ in various respects from our own, so that diagrammatic tests may present quite unforeseen problems to them. We are apt to forget also the importance of the testee's attitude or 'sets' (cf. p. 73), since we have become so used, as school children, to answering silly questions put to us by adults as quickly as possible. In addition to educational handicaps, the African may do badly on tests devised by Europeans because this attitude of competition and rapid response is unnatural to his culture. Even as near home as the Hebridean islands, it was found that the more leisurely tempo of the children's lives greatly affected their responses to intelligence tests given in Gaelic (Smith, 1948). Again, among Australian natives the accepted reaction to difficult problems is group consultation, not individual effort. These natives are in many respects highly 'intelligent' in relation to their barren environment, though obviously backward by European standards. It is for such reasons that psychologists like Biesheuvel, together with most anthropologists, regard attempts to compare the intelligence of different cultural groups as futile.

If we are to make progress it is likely that verbal tests, preferably given orally in the vernacular, provide a better medium than any other, since language is a universal instrument for the handling of complex intellectual problems. Reasonable comparisons might be made between pairs of groups whose modes of thought, grammar and syntax have been shown, by anthropological and linguistic studies, to be closely similar; for we might then be able to construct tests which presented comparable problems to members of each group.

These somewhat pessimistic conclusions do not imply that intelligence and other tests cannot be useful within groups other than western European and American. They can be, and have been, constructed and applied for educational and vocational selection and other purposes in many parts of Africa and India. Biesheuvel, for example, has an extensive battery of performance and manual tests for South African mineworkers which are given in group form with cinematograph demonstrations of what the testees have to do. A particularly illuminating piece of work is Scott's (1950) production of group verbal tests for selection for intermediate and secondary schools in the Sudan. An oral test, based on Ballard's, was devised for the former level (about 11 years), and a written one, based on Moray House, for the latter (about 16 years). But straight translations of these models into Arabic were useless. Many of the original items aroused quite different associations among Sudanese pupils, and only after lengthy experimentation with some 900 items were sufficient suitable ones obtained. Scott also found it necessary to introduce a lengthy process of 'warming up' or preliminary practice, and to give much more time than in an English setting. But satisfactory reliability coefficients and correlations with subsequent educational success were eventually achieved.

Chapter Eleven

EDUCATIONAL AND VOCATIONAL
IMPLICATIONS OF INTELLIGENCE TESTS

FACTOR ANALYSIS

SOME summing up of the results of factorial studies is desirable before we consider the relevance of intelligence tests to educational and vocational guidance and selection. It was shown in Chapter One that one of the most fruitful sources of information on what tests measure is an analysis of the way they tend to group together. If a dozen tests, A, B, . . . L are given to the same testees, and the correlations of A, C, D and F with one another are higher than with the remainder, we can observe the common features in these tests which are not present in the others and deduce the nature of the group factor that is operating. The appropriate statistical techniques developed by Spearman, Burt and Thurstone enable us to measure how much of the general factor, which runs through the whole battery and of this or other group factors, are present in each test and how much is specific.

The following seem to be the main factors involved in the tests which we have described in Chapters Four to Six.

g. We have shown that *g* cannot be identified with any clearcut mental faculty, but is rather the common element remaining once the group factors present in all tests have been allowed for; also that it is likely to differ in nature among younger and older children and adults. A further complication is that it is always most prominent in heterogeneous populations such as a complete age-group of children or unselected adult recruits, but may almost vanish if a selected group of narrow ability range is studied, such as university students or Army officers (hence the preference of Thurstone, Guilford and other American factorists for analysing abilities entirely in terms of group factors). Very probably, again, *g* is more pronounced among low-grade populations; thus manual and mental tests tend to inter-correlate more highly among defectives.

Nevertheless, we can agree with Spearman that it is something in the nature of grasping relationships, and is most strongly evident in tests of the more complex intellectual functions such as reasoning and abstraction, in the learning of classics and in problem arithmetic. Indeed, it is just as plausible to analyse the main factors present in ordinary intelligence tests into Thurstone's R (reasoning) $+ V$ factors as into $g+$ a verbal group factor. It is less prominent in more rote abilities such as memorisation, mechanical ability and occupational skills, and (within the normal range) is almost absent in manual and physical capacities. But there are no pure g tests, and even the Terman-Merrill, or verbal abstraction tests or non-verbal tests like Progressive Matrices, do not involve more than about 50 per cent of g.

v. The verbal factor enters into all verbal tests such as vocabulary, analogies, reading comprehension, spelling, etc., over and above g, and is so largely dependent on schooling that the writer refers to it elsewhere as the $v:ed$ factor (Vernon, 1950). Particularly among unselected adults it tends to interact so closely with g that it is difficult to distinguish general intelligence from amount of education received. But in more selected groups—grammar school pupils, for example—it may differentiate into a number of factors along the lines of different school subjects. Thus, most pupils who are above average in English composition will also be good in foreign languages because of their common g and v content, but some may be relatively stronger in one than the other, indicating the influence of minor specialised abilities. Verbal psychological tests can similarly be classified under partially distinct factors of verbal comprehension, fluency, induction and deduction, concept-formation, etc., and—at the highest levels— under Guilford's long list of evaluative, planning, creativity and other factors. However, there is no general agreement yet among factorists as to the number and precise specification of these subfactors.

n, or number ability, likewise tends to overlap with the verbal-educational factor. It is most clearly present in mechanical arithmetic tests. More advanced arithmetic and mathematics bring in a larger g component; and at secondary or higher levels there is likely to be some differentiation of geometrical, scientific and other specialised abilities.

$k:m$ and S. Earlier writers identified a k (kinæsthetic) factor in tests involving the manipulation of shapes in the imagination, and an m (mechanical) factor either in tests of a practical-constructional type or in those based on pictures of mechanisms. Mechanical ability, however, seems to resolve almost completely into k on the one hand and knowledge of, or experience with, mechanical things on the other. Physical capacities and manual dexterities also overlap with this factor, though they are largely specific. For example, quickness in screwing up nuts and bolts correlates little with speed of running or reaction time, or with ability at a formboard test like the Goddard; and none of these agree at all closely with any trade skill. Thus $k:m$ stands for the complex which we call practical, as contrasted with academic or $v:ed$ factor. The more difficult performance tests such as Kohs Blocks and Cube Construction measure the same k ability as paper-and-pencil spatial tests (together with g and specific factors); thus they are useful vocationally. But the simpler picture and formboard tests are mostly rather unreliable g tests with large specific components. Hence, as we have pointed out, even a reliable battery cannot claim any special relevance to intelligence in practical daily-life activities, and is definitely inferior for educational predictions. Group tests based on pictures or diagrams likewise measure no very clear factors apart from g and specifics, though sometimes showing a small k component when spatial imagery enters.

The S factor of American writers is much the same as k, but in this area, too, they often break it down into several partially distinct abilities. Guilford, for instance, finds a Visualisation factor which he contrasts with Spatial Relations Ability.

M. Thurstone and others have found a distinct rote memory factor in tests involving the learning and immediate reproduction of non-meaningful material (digits, nonsense syllables, shapes, etc.). This has little or no bearing on school work, and meaningful learning is almost wholly a matter of g and v, and specialised ability at or interest in the particular subject.

X. Attainment tests and school marks and examinations always show closer overlapping with one another than with intelligence tests, and this has been attributed by Alexander (1935) to an industriousness factor, which he calls X. But X is not merely a character trait among the pupils; it combines all the influences, such as parental encouragement, good teaching, etc., which differentiate a pupil's E.Q. from his I.Q. Nor can we, in fact, measure X independently; personality tests and ratings by teachers of the children or of home conditions are not yet sufficiently accurate to be of much practical value (cf. Vernon, 1953). However, it is useful to realise, in educational selection, that we do need to assess: $g + v + n + X$. Intelligence tests do not cover X at all; standardised attainment tests do so to some extent, but not so well as the more orthodox type of school examination or teachers' estimates of attainments and promise.

Formal Factors and Conditions of Work. When ordinary group intelligence tests, based mainly on choice-response items, are compared with creative-response group or individual tests, the former show a distinct factor, presumably representing facility at this rather artificial type of question. Very likely it is involved, too, in English attainment, reading comprehension, and other new-type tests. Probably it is for this reason that school teachers often find group test results conflicting with their observations of pupils' abilities and criticise them for measuring 'slickness'.[1] Actually they do largely depend on g and v, but bring in this irrelevant component as well. The Terman-Merrill avoids it. and so appears to give a more valid indication of intelligence at school and in daily life, although it is less scientifically constructed than many group tests.

Next we must consider the influence of speed of work in tests given with a time-limit. This has been a topic of controversy ever since the first American Army tests were constructed. Ballard (1922) criticised their emphasis on speed, and many educationists have expressed similar opinions. Most psychologists, however, finding extremely close agreement between the results of speeded and unspeeded tests, have disputed this and have followed the American model, largely because it is much simpler to invent easy than difficult test items and much more convenient administratively if all testees finish tests at the same moment. Actually, almost all group tests involve 'speed' *and* 'power'. The first half of the items may be done rapidly and without much thought by the bright pupil, but his g and v mainly determine his capacity at the final band of items where he reaches his limit; while the less bright pupil manages a quarter or less at speed and then needs all his g and v to score on some of the middle band.

[1] There are several other reasons, of course, such as the teacher's failure to allow for the child's chronological age and his tendency to confuse ability with moral character, perseverance and likeability.

More recent researches reveal various motor speed factors, or quickness at manual and other tasks, also P—perceptual speed (cf. p. 86)—but give little support to the notion of a general mental speed or slickness, as contrasted with more 'profound' ability. Rather it appears that certain *attitudes to work* are involved at different levels of difficulty. If a mental test consists entirely of rather easy items and the score is based on number correct in a given time, some pupils or adults will concentrate mainly on speed at the expense of accuracy, some the reverse. On the other hand, if the test consists of difficult questions with no time-limit, the score will depend as much on persistence at that type of material as on intellectual ability (cf. Mangan, 1959). Testing at either of these two extremes is not very suitable for intelligence measurement or for educational prediction, since the results are too greatly affected by the testee's motivation and attitude to the test. Hence the majority of group tests fall roughly in the middle range of difficulty. However, in the writer's judgment our present tests for secondary school selection are inclined somewhat too far to the Speed *v*. Accuracy type, and might with advantage include more difficult problems and more generous time-limits. This may be another reason why the unspeeded Terman-Merrill test appears to give such useful results. Similarly, in arithmetic, Sutherland (1952) found slightly better predictions of secondary school work from tests with longer time-limits. But we should not jump to the conclusion that timed tests select the careless and untimed the persistent pupil; the attitudes involved in such tests are highly complex and probably bear little relation to the attitudes involved in slipshod and careful school work. And we must insist that tests given under these different conditions nevertheless measure very largely the same combination of g, v, n or other abilities.

INTELLIGENCE TESTS AND EDUCATION

We are now in a position to understand more clearly the educational uses of intelligence tests. A good individual test applied between $5\frac{1}{2}$ and $9\frac{1}{2}$, or a thorough group test given from about 10 onwards, mainly measures the same g and v factors that enter into all-round school attainment. We can no longer claim that they show innate intelligence or capacity for learning; but since they depend on level of concept development and generalised

thinking skills they should, in most cases, also give an indication
of the level of school work that children are capable of tackling.
And in so far as they are somewhat less affected than are measures
of attainment by good or poor teaching, environmental handicaps
or advantages, temperamental factors and emotional adjustment,
they can be interpreted as showing educational potentiality. At
the same time we must remember that conditions that improve or
harm attainment may also quite likely affect intelligence test
results, even if in lesser degree.

The correlation between $g + v$ tests and general attainment is
very high, at least in a primary school age-group—approximating
0·85. Nevertheless, this allows of considerable discrepancies in individual cases. Such discrepancies would be expected both because of
the imperfect reliability of the tests or assessments and because
each includes some different group factors. The complex of conditions that we called the X-factor, together with specialised
abilities at particular subjects, enter into attainment, and the
irrelevant formal factors, discussed above, often affect intelligence
tests. Thus a child's I.Q. may be lower than his E.Q. if he is
relatively poor in answering multiple-choice questions at speed, or
if he is strongly interested in school and well taught so that his
English and number skills are in advance of his wider thinking
capacities. Again, if the E.Q. falls markedly below the I.Q., this
does not necessarily show serious retardation (cf. p. 120) attributable to environmental or temperamental handicaps: the form or
content of the intelligence test may happen to suit him. In other
words, differences between 'intelligence' and 'attainments' are
very much on a par with differences between arithmetic and
reading, or any other highly correlated abilities. They *may* be a
sign of special difficulties which require psychological treatment
or remedial education, but they may also be due to a variety of
other causes.

The greater the influence of other group factors, naturally the
bigger the discrepancies. Thus mechanical arithmetic, handwriting
and manual subjects are least well predicted by intelligence tests
because of their low $g + v$ content (cf. Burt, 1939). For the same
reason, pictorial, performance, or abstract non-verbal tests with
no v-content—while excellent for experimental research purposes where it is desired to isolate a non-verbal g factor—are of
relatively little educational or vocational value. However, there is

some evidence that non-verbal group tests may be rather more predictive of ability in technical and scientific subjects at the secondary stage than are verbal tests (cf. p. 90). It is particularly unwise to use them as a criterion of educational potentiality, except possibly among deaf or non-English-speaking pupils; (even among the latter, a verbal test in their mother tongue, plus a test of such English as they have already acquired, is likely to give a better indication of their capacity for acquiring an education in English).

Note that this view in no way detracts from the usefulness of intelligence tests for selection purposes. The potential grammar school pupil requires high-level thinking skills as well as good attainments in the basic subjects. But it does involve some re-orientation in current applications of tests for educational guidance. The clinic or educational psychologist should clearly not rely on I.Q.–E.Q. discrepancy to pick the cases most likely to benefit from remedial treatment. The teacher's subjective judgment that Johnny 'could do better' or is 'under-functioning' in school, is likely to be as good a guide, though this needs, of course, to be supplemented by a thorough investigation of the personality, home, schooling and other relevant circumstances.

In the secondary grammar school, intelligence tests show a much lower relation to all-round school work, mainly because of the greater homogeneity (the high degree of selection) of the pupils, though also because specialised talents are developing. They continue to provide a useful indication of intellectual level in the modern school, where the range of ability is much wider. For the same reason they give moderately useful predictions in American colleges and universities, with their heterogeneous intakes (cf. Eysenck, 1947), but show very little correspondence with university success in Britain—correlations of 0·2 to 0·3. The enormous majority of British university students obtain I.Q.s in the 115 to 150 range, and Honours graduates score higher on the average than Pass degree ones. But occasional students may achieve successful careers with I.Q.s down to 100, and there is little evidence that tests of the conventional type could improve on the selection of students by means of secondary school examination performance. Nevertheless, better prognostic tests of verbal comprehension and reasoning in different branches of study, such as are generally used in America (cf. p. 25), could certainly be devised if university selecting bodies gave any encouragement to the psychologist (cf. Himmelweit and Summerfield, 196).

It is sometimes argued that British universities could and should be greatly expanded because there are so many individuals in the general population with I.Q.s as good as those of most students, whose talent is being wasted. But the correlation is so low that this argument is little better than saying that—since university students tend to be taller than average, therefore all men of 6 ft. and over should go to university. The supply of suitable students depends much more on a combination of the following factors than on the I.Q. distribution:

(i) The educational and vocational aspirations of the family; its expectation that the children will undertake an arduous educational career and eventually enter high-level jobs, and the material and moral support it provides towards these ends.

(ii) The child's own drives, interests and ideals.

(iii) The traditions and current attitudes in the schools the child attends, and in society generally, and the prestige of occupations requiring university training.

(iv) The effectiveness of teachers and teaching methods in developing favourable attitudes among pupils towards the academic subjects and education generally.

Modern conceptions of intelligence and its testing also require some revision of our notions of streaming, or the segregation of brighter and duller pupils (cf. Vernon, 1957). In the 1920s much was heard of the tremendously wide range of Mental Ages among children in a typical school class, and of the advantages of homogeneous grouping or streaming. It was said that, when children are grouped mainly by age, the bright ones are apt to become lazy or conceited and the dull ones depressed and resentful. Moreover, this diversity increases the higher up the school: in a 6-year class about $13\frac{1}{2}$ per cent of pupils were intellectually equipped to do the work of the classes one year or more in advance, and $13\frac{1}{2}$ per cent capable only of the work of classes one year younger. But at 12 years, the proportions so misplaced would be likely to reach 29 per cent.

However, grouping by M.A. would obviously involve an enormously wide Chronological Age range in each class; there would be serious social difficulties if, say, bright 5- or 6-year olds were taught along with dull 9- or 10-year olds. Hence it was thought better to aim at three streams—the bright, the average and the dull—in each age-group; so that any one class would contain pupils all of nearly the same age *and* of a limited range of M.A.

For a number of reasons this policy is less favoured nowadays, particularly in primary schools.

1. Clearly it cannot be applied in the vast number of small schools which take in only 30 to 40 children or less per year.

2. Inevitably it has bad effects on the morale of the children and their parents, since it is impossible to conceal from the duller groups that they are regarded as failures; and this inhibits their interest in educational progress.

3. There is grave danger of any classificatory system becoming unduly rigid, and thus neglecting the considerable fluctuations in abilities and interests which we have seen to be characteristic of mental growth. Even the most successful schemes of secondary school selection relegate some 5 per cent of children to modern schools who could later have done work of grammar school standard and admit another 5 per cent who are relatively unfitted. Too often in the primary school, also, children are classified soon after entry, and the A's are brought on so much more rapidly that the B's and C's soon lose any chance of catching up. We can, however, calculate that in such a three-stream primary school, only about two-thirds should be expected to stay in the same ability stream throughout, and some 10 per cent are likely to merit reclassification every year, i.e. to shift up or down one or even two streams.

Insufficient flexibility in school organisation is at least as serious at the bottom as at the top of the ability range. Suppose that it were possible to segregate 5 per cent of the most backward at any one time in special schools or classes, then we can calculate that only about $1\frac{1}{2}$ per cent are likely to remain in this subnormal group throughout their primary school careers. On the other hand, as many as one-quarter of the total would at some stage in their schooling merit inclusion in the backward group. Figures such as these clearly point to the desirability of temporary backward classes, as against the traditional policy of removing educationally subnormal and defective children more or less permanently into special schools.

4. We have pointed out many times that success in any school subject involves other factors besides the $g + v$ measured by

intelligence tests. There is no justification for the argument that Mental Age provides a more fundamental measure of potentiality than do other kinds of assessment. Thus, if we must stream, it would be better to base it on a combination of average attainments, intelligence and teachers' assessments, just as we do in selection at 11-plus, and as is, in fact, usually done in the ascertainment of E.S.N. pupils. But even if a class is homogeneous in general promise, we must expect to find much greater variations among its members in particular subjects or in branches of a subject. It can never be homogeneous for everything. This, of course, is often recognised at the secondary level and partially met by cross-classification or setting for mathematics, foreign languages, etc.

Nevertheless, this objection to grouping is sometimes exaggerated. Actually the general factors in attainment $(g + v + X)$ in the primary and secondary modern school tend to be much more prominent than group factors. Thus the proposal of the Norwood Report to classify children according to their *type* of ability—academic, technical or practical—was totally unrealistic (cf. Burt, 1943*a*), since success among 11–15 year olds at almost any curriculum depends mainly on the same combination of abilities, personality traits and home backing. Provided, then, that sufficent flexibility can be maintained, class organisation on a basis of general suitability is educationally sound. The wise teacher can readily cater for special talents within such classes, for example by using a boy's relative superiority at handwork, stamp collecting or social leadership to boost his morale and encourage his application to the more formal subjects in which he is relatively inferior.

5. Finally, we must ask whether there is any evidence that streaming within schools, or segregation into schools at different levels of ability, produces superior results to non-streaming. Several American researches indicate that over the whole range of the school population there are no measurable advantages. At the same time it is virtually certain that the extreme ends of the distribution of ability do benefit from teaching by specially trained staff, using methods adapted to superior, or to very inferior, pupils. Imbeciles and idiots must clearly be segregated, and the 1 to 2 per cent of higher-grade defectives seem to make better progress in E.S.N. schools or special classes than in ordinary schools. There is indeed a strong case for expanding backward classes to

allow remedial work with, say, the 5 per cent most backward, provided always that transfer to and from such classes is easy.

At the other end of the scale, there is no doubt that grammar and public school pupils make better progress in segregated schools or segregated streams within the comprehensive school. Such advanced subjects as mathematics, English grammar, classics or history can probably be tackled with profit only by the 10 to 15 per cent most able pupils. But the stage at which segregation should occur, and the most appropriate type of school organisation which will cater for this group, without denying opportunities to later developers, are matters of educational values and policy rather than of psychology and mental measurement. The most we can infer from psychometric evidence is that there should probably be less rather than more streaming within secondary, and even less within primary, schools. It is likely that the full realisation of each individual's potentialities can be better brought about by extending individual and small-group work within a heterogeneous class than by class-teaching of 30, 40 or more children all belonging to a restricted range of ability.

INTELLIGENCE TESTS AND VOCATIONAL SUITABILITY

When intelligence tests are applied to adults in various jobs, very considerable differentiation may be observed according to the degree of intellectual ability and the length of training that the jobs involve. Fig. 8 shows some results collected for 10,000 Army recruits in 1939–40 by Himmelweit and Whitfield (1944), using a 10-minute verbal test. Scores have been converted to equivalent I.Q.s by the writer. Each occupational group includes 120 or more cases. The middle line in each bar represents the median score, and the ends of the bar the 90th and 10th percentiles. For example, all but the top and bottom 10 per cent of those who were labourers in civil life fall between I.Q. 73 and 106. Now, while the average school-teacher obtains a much higher I.Q. than the average labourer, it will be seen that there is considerable overlapping. Indeed, some of the highest 10 per cent of labourers are apparently more intelligent than some of the lowest 10 per cent of teachers. It is likely that the professional persons of lowish intelligence would be rather slow in passing their courses, and that the highly intelligent labourers may be dissatisfied with the intellectual content of their jobs. But researches dealing with

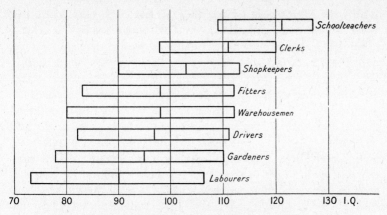

FIG. 8 Range of I.Q.s (from 10th to 90th Percentiles) among
Recruits from Certain Occupations.

particular occupations show that, within limits, too low (or too
high) intelligence is not necessarily a sign of incapacity or in-
efficiency. In other words, a school-leaver's I.Q. will give us a
general picture of the *level* of job for which he is likely to be
suited. But the correlation with success in any one job is usually
too slight for any accurate prediction. Again, intelligence tests
alone show nothing about the relative suitability of different
types of job—involving different specialised abilities and interests
—at any one level.

Another qualification is needed. The fact that some groups, such
as teachers, generally show above average intelligence, does not
prove that people could not do this work with a lower score.
Entry to the profession is restricted mainly to young people with
successful secondary school records. Also teaching is a common
choice for the bright leaver who has no strong talents or inclinations for other careers, or little opportunity for gaining a foothold
in them. Thus we do not really know to what extent the present
distribution of teacher I.Q.s is artificially boosted. Other jobs, for
similar reasons, may be failing to attract as good a range of
intelligence as they need.

Nevertheless, we have shown elsewhere (Vernon and Parry,
1949) that intelligence tests do sometimes give useful indications
of vocational suitability. First, they correlate moderately well with
proficiency at clerical jobs, or other work that involves dealing

with words and figures. They are least related to jobs where the work is highly specialised (e.g. radio), where manual skills are involved, or where personality qualities are of greater importance than intellectual skills or knowledge (e.g. business or teaching). Secondly, they are very valuable when, as in the Armed Forces, rapid trainability, and in particular the capacity to learn mechanical, electrical or other theory, are important. Thirdly, much depends on the degree of heterogeneity of the candidates. If these are pre-selected on educational or other grounds, intelligence tests have little to contribute. But when, again as in the Services, a very wide range of ability occurs, they certainly help in allocating brighter recruits to more skilled employments. In civilian life they can, for example, be given with advantage to intending nurses, who may not only be very heterogeneous in background but also have a lot of theory to learn. At the same time they will predict success only moderately well, since personality qualities obviously play such a large part in good nursing. In general, tests should certainly be used in vocational guidance of modern school-leavers (the 11-plus results are *not* adequate at 14+), but are less necessary with grammar school-leavers whose academic record is known.

A surprising finding during the war was that the purer non-verbal tests of g were generally less useful in predicting occupational abilities than tests with an obvious educational bias—that is, tests of $g + v$. Indeed, a test of arithmetic and mathematics was the most useful of all, not only for clerical and technical jobs but for predicting all-round efficiency. Spatial tests and mechanical comprehension and information ($k:m$) certainly had a contribution to make in the selection of mechanics, but in almost all jobs the main requirement was that same complex of qualities that grammar schools look for at 11-plus (cf. p. 181). More specialised tests of group factors, indeed, were seldom of much value in allocating recruits to suitable jobs, when a very wide variety of possibilities existed. The same is likely to be true in vocational *guidance* of school-leavers. Vocational *selection* is different. When the psychologist wishes to pick the best candidates for one par-ticular job, he should proceed to analyse the aptitudes and qualities involved and test them by an appropriately designed battery of tests. But the usefulness of tests in guidance has often been ex-aggerated. General intelligence and educational level should be determined; supplementary mechanical-spatial tests (for boys) and clerical tests are often worth adding. But much more attention should be paid to interests, relevant experience and opportunities, home background, physical assets and weaknesses and personality qualities.

A final caution may be in place against over-valuating intelligence as measured by tests. Because this book has attempted to answer misinformed or prejudiced critics, it has naturally stressed such evidence as that of Terman and the high correlations with secondary school success. But most of the world's work is carried out by men and women of around average intelligence. The intelligent adult or child is not, as some people seem to suspect, socially *un*desirable in any way that we can discern, but he is also not the only desirable citizen.

APPENDIX: ANSWERS TO EXAMPLES

7. elbow
8. 23   30
9. TRUE
10. OPPOSITE
11. SAME
12. R
14. harmony
15. avoid
16. nightingale
17. perfunctory meticulous
18. fish
19. a door
20. Fireplace
21. GHV
22. the fourth figure
23. cottonwool flour
24. the third figure
25. second minute
26. 32
27. the third figure
28. sun summer winter
29. 2 Stephen
30. + +   — + —
31. sacrifice object
32. FALSE
33. SOME
34. SILLY
37. Kathleen
38. Yes
39. north
41. WEEK
42. 52
43. E
45. Kamala(m) Monoharam
46. h
47. O X blank O

48. the fourth figure
49. the first figure
50. Summer (or New Year Christmas)
51. 7643
52. foal
53. sun
54. 381191
55. No. 4
56. the second figure
57. the fourth figure
58. the third figure
59. 24
60. 5
63. Nos. 1, 6, 8 squares
    2, 4, 5 upright rectangles
    3, 7, 9 sideways rectangles
    1, 3, 5, 8 unshaded
    2, 6, 9 half-shaded
    4, 7 shaded
65. the second answer
66. ·4771
67. mediocre
72. were
73. gave
75. cow
76. audacious
77. wheels
78–79. Any complete, grammatical sentences
80. was stolen from the larder by Jim
81. if she could go

BIBLIOGRAPHY

BOOKS or articles which are starred (*) are recommended for further reading.

ALEXANDER, W. P. (1935). Intelligence, Concrete and Abstract. *Brit. J. Psychol. Monogr.*, No. 19.

ALLPORT, G. W. (1954). *The Nature of Prejudice.* Cambridge, Mass.: Addison-Wesley.

*ANASTASI, A. (1954). *Psychological Testing.* New York: Macmillan.

*ANASTASI, A. (1958). *Differential Psychology.* New York: Macmillan.

ANSTEY, E. (1948). The *d* Method of Item Analysis. *Brit. J. Statist. Psychol.*, 1, 167–177.

BALDWIN, A. L., KALHORN, J. and BREESE, F. H. (1945). Patterns of Parent Behavior. *Psychol. Monogr.*, 58, No. 268.

BALLARD, P. B. (1920). *Mental Tests.* University of London Press.

BALLARD, P. B. (1922). *Group Tests of Intelligence.* University of London Press.

BALLARD, P. B. (1923). *The New Examiner.* University of London Press.

BALLER, W. R. (1936). A Study of the Present Social Status of a Group of Adults who, when They Were in Elementary Schools, Were Classified as Mentally Deficient. *Genet. Psychol. Monogr.*, 18, 165–244.

BANKS, C. and BURT, C. (1953). Statistical Analysis in Educational Psychology. *Current Trends in British Psychology* (ed. C. A. Mace and P. E. Vernon), 152–171. Methuen.

*BARTLETT, F. C. (1958.) *Thinking.* Allen and Unwin.

BAYLEY, N. (1940). Mental Growth in Young Children. *Thirty-ninth Yrbk. Nat. Soc. Stud. Educ.*, Pt. II, 11–47. Bloomington, Ill.: Public School Publishing Co.

BERLYNE, D. E. (1957). Recent Developments in Piaget's Work. *Brit. J. Educ. Psychol.*, 27, 1–12.

*BIESHEUVEL, S. (1949). Psychological Tests and their Application to Non-European Peoples. *Yrbk. of Educ.*, 87–126. Evans Bros.

BLACK, E. L. (1954). The Difficulties of Training College Students in Understanding What They Read. *Brit. J. Educ. Psychol.*, 24, 17–31.

BLANDFORD, J. S. (1958). Standardised Tests in Junior Schools with Special Reference to the Effects of Streaming on the Constancy of Results. *Brit. J. Educ. Psychol.*, 28, 170–173.

BOARD OF EDUCATION (1924). *Psychological Tests of Educable Capacity and their Possible Use in the Public System of Education.* Report of Consultative Committee, H.M.S.O.

BROLYER, C. R., THORNDIKE, E. L. and WOODYARD, E. (1927). A Second Study of Mental Discipline in High School Students. *J. Educ. Psychol.*, 18, 377–404.

BÜHLER, C. and HETZER, H. (1935). *Testing Children's Development from Birth to School Age.* Allen and Unwin.

*BUROS, O. K. (1959). *The Fifth Mental Measurements Yearbook.* Highland Park, New Jersey: Gryphon Press.

BURT, C. (1921). *Mental and Scholastic Tests.* King.

BURT, C. (1925). *Northumberland Standardised Tests 1, 2 and 3.* University of London Press.

BURT, C. (1925a). *The Young Delinquent.* University of London Press.

BURT, C. (1939). The Relations of Educational Abilities. *Brit. J. Educ. Psychol.,* **9,** 45–71.

BURT, C. (1943). Ability and Income. *Brit. J. Educ. Psychol.,* **13,** 83–98.

BURT, C. (1943a). The Education of the Young Adolescent: Psychological Implications of the Norwood Report. *Brit. J. Educ. Psychol.,* **13,** 126–140.

BURT, C. (1946). *Intelligence and Fertility.* Eugenics Society.

*BURT, C. (1955). The Evidence for the Concept of Intelligence. *Brit. J. Educ. Psychol.,* **25,** 158–177.

BURT, C. (1955a). *The Subnormal Mind* (3rd edit.). Oxford University Press.

BURT, C. (1957). The Distribution of Intelligence. *Brit. J. Psychol.,* **48,** 161–174.

CATTELL, P. (1940). *Intelligence Scale for Infants and Young Children.* New York: Psychological Corporation.

CATTELL, R. B. (1934). Occupational Norms of Intelligence and the Standardisation of an Adult Intelligence Test. *Brit. J. Psychol.,* **25,** 1–28.

CATTELL, R. B. (1935). *Intelligence Scales.* Harrap.

CATTELL, R. B. (1949–50). *Tests of G: Culture Free.* Champaign, Ill.: Institute for Personality and Ability Testing.

CATTELL, R. B. and VERNON, P. E. (1937). Articles in *Char. & Person.,* **6,** 99–131.

CHARLES, D. C. (1953). Ability and Accomplishment of Persons Earlier Judged Mentally Defective. *Genet. Psychol. Monogr.,* **47,** 3–71.

*CLARKE, A. M. and CLARKE, A. D. B. (1958). *Mental Deficiency: the Changing Outlook.* Methuen.

COHEN, S. W. (1949). *Cohen French Tests.* Melbourne: Australian Council for Educational Research.

CONNOR, D. V. (1952). *The Effect of Temperamental Traits upon Intelligence Test Responses.* Ph.D. Thesis, University of London Library.

CONRAD, H. S. and JONES, H. E. (1940). A Second Study of Familial Resemblances in Intelligence. *Thirty-ninth Yrbk. Nat. Soc. Stud. Educ.,* Pt. II, 97–141. Bloomington, Ill.: Public School Publishing Co.

COOK, W. W. (1932). The Measurement of General Spelling Ability Involving Controlled Comparison between Techniques. *Univ. Iowa Stud. Educ.,* No. 6.

CORNWELL, J. (1952). *An Orally Presented Group Test of Intelligence for Juniors.* Methuen.

CRANE, A. R. (1959). An Historical and Critical Account of the Accomplishment Quotient Idea. *Brit. J. Educ. Psychol.,* **29,** 252–259.

*CRONBACH, L. J. (1949). *Essentials of Psychological Testing.* New York: Harper.

CRONBACH, L. J. and GLESER, G. C. (1958). *Psychological Tests and Personnel Decisions.* Urbana, Ill.: University of Illinois Press.

CURETON, E. E. (1937). The Accomplishment Quotient Technic. *J. Exper. Educ.,* **5,** 315–326.

CURR, W. and GOURLAY, N. (1953). An Experimental Evaluation of Remedial Education. *Brit. J. Educ. Psychol.,* **23,** 45–55.

DANIELS, J. C. and DIACK, H. (1958). *The Standard Reading Tests.* Chatto and Windus.

DAWSON, S. (1936). Environmental Influences on Mentality. *Brit. J. Psychol.*, **27,** 129–134.

DEARBORN, W. F. and ROTHNEY, J. W. M. (1941). *Predicting the Child's Development.* Cambridge, Mass.: Sci-Art.

DEWAR, H. (1938). A Comparison of Tests of Artistic Appreciation. *Brit. J. Educ. Psychol.*, **8,** 29–49.

DREVER, J. and COLLINS, M. (1936). *Performance Tests of Intelligence* (2nd edit.). Edinburgh: Oliver and Boyd.

DUFF, J. F. and THOMSON, G. H. (1923). The Social and Geographical Distribution of Intelligence in Northumberland. *Brit. J. Psychol.*, **14,** 192–198.

EARLE, F. M. (1948). *The Duplex Series of Ability Tests.* Harrap.

EELLS, K., HAVIGHURST, R. J. et al. (1951). *Intelligence and Cultural Differences.* University of Chicago Press.

EMMETT, W. G. (1954). The Intelligence of Urban and Rural Children. *Population Stud.*, **7,** 207–221.

EYSENCK, H. J. (1947). Student Selection by Means of Psychological Tests. *Brit. J. Educ. Psychol.*, **17,** 20–39.

FERGUSON, G. A. (1954). On Learning and Human Ability. *Canad. J. Psychol.*, **8,** 95–112.

FLEMING, C. M., *Kelvin Arithmetic Test*, and *Cotswold Junior Ability Tests.* Glasgow: Gibson.

FLEMING, C. M. (1943). Socio-economic Level and Test Performance. *Brit. J. Educ. Psychol.*, **13,** 74–82.

FOULDS, C. A. and RAVEN, J. C. (1948). Normal Changes in the Mental Abilities of Adults as Age Advances. *J. Ment. Sci.*, **94,** 135–142.

GAW, F. (1925). Performance Tests of Intelligence. *Industr. Fat. Res. Board Rep.*, No. 31. H.M.S.O.

GESELL, A. and AMATRUDA, C. S. (1947). *Developmental Diagnosis.* New York: Hoeber.

GIBBENS, T. C. N. (1958). The Porteus Maze Test and Delinquency. *Brit. J. Educ. Psychol.*, **28,** 209–216.

GOODENOUGH, F. L. (1926). *Measurement of Intelligence by Drawings.* Harrap.

GORDON, H. (1923). Mental and Scholastic Tests Among Retarded Children. *Board of Educ. Pamphl.* No. 44. H.M.S.O.

GRAY, J. L. and MOSHINSKI, P. (1936). *The Nation's Intelligence.* Watts.

GREENE, K. B. (1928). The Influence of Specialized Training on Tests of General Intelligence. *Twenty-seventh Yrbk. Nat. Soc. Stud. Educ.*, 421–428. Bloomington, Ill.: Public School Publishing Co.

★GRIFFITHS, R. (1954). *The Abilities of Babies.* University of London Press.

★GUILFORD, J. P. (1956). The Structure of Intellect. *Psychol. Bull.*, **53,** 267–293.

HALSEY, A. H. (1958). Genetics, Social Structure and Intelligence. *Brit. J. Sociol.*, **9,** 15–28.

HARLOW, H. F. (1949). The Formation of Learning Sets. *Psychol. Rev.*, **56,** 51–65.

★HEBB, D. O. (1948). *The Organization of Behavior.* New York: Wiley.

HEIM, A. W. (1954). *The Appraisal of Intelligence.* Methuen.

HEIM, A. W., *Tests AH4 and AH5.* National Foundation for Educational Research.

HEIM, A. W. *et al.* (1949–50). The Effects of Repeatedly Retesting the Same Group on the Same Intelligence Test. *Quart. J. Exper. Psychol.*, **1**, 151–159; **2**, 19–32, 182–195.

HIGHFIELD, M. E., *Southend Attainment Test in Mechanical Arithmetic*. Harrap.

HIGHFIELD, M. E. (1954). *Kingston Test of Silent Reading*. Harrap.

HIMMELWEIT, H. T. and SUMMERFIELD, A. (1951). Student Selection: An Experimental Investigation, II. *Brit. J. Sociol*, **2**, 59–75.

HIMMELWEIT, H. T. and WHITFIELD, J. W. (1949). Mean Intelligence Scores of a Random Sample of Occupations. *Brit. J. Industr. Med.*, **1**, 224–226.

HUSÉN, T. (1951). The Influence of Schooling upon I.Q. *Theoria*, **17**, 61–88.

JENKINS, J. W. (1947). *A Scale of Non-verbal Mental Ability*. National Foundation for Educational Research.

JONES, T. *et al.*, (1952). A Group Performance Test Scale of Intelligence. *Brit. J. Educ. Psychol.*, **22**, 160–172.

KEATS, J. A. (1950). *A Statistical Theory of Objective Test Scores*. Melbourne: Australian Council for Educational Research (mimeographed).

KENNEDY FRASER, D. (1945). *The Terman-Merrill Intelligence Scale in Scotland*. University of London Press.

KLINEBERG, O. (1935). *Negro Intelligence and Selective Migration*. New York: Columbia University Press.

*KNIGHT, R. (1943). *Intelligence and Intelligence Tests* (2nd edit.). Methuen.

KOHS, S. C. (1923). *Intelligence Measurement*. New York: Macmillan.

LAMBERT, C. M. (1951). *Seven Plus Assessment*. University of London Press.

LAWRENCE, E. M. (1931). An Investigation into the Relationship between Intelligence and Environment. *Brit. J. Psychol. Monogr.* No. 16.

LEARNED, W. S. and WOOD, B. P. (1938). *The Student and His Knowledge*. New York: Carnegie Foundation.

*LINDQUIST, E. F. (ed.) (1951). *Educational Measurement*. Washington, D.C.: American Council on Education.

LORD, F. M. (1955). Some Perspectives in 'The Attenuation Paradox in Test Theory'. *Psychol. Bull.*, **52**, 505–510.

LORGE, I. (1955). Schooling Makes a Difference. *Teach. Coll. Rec.*, **46**, 483–492.

LOVELL, K. (1955). Intellectual Deterioration in Adolescents and Young Adults. *Brit. J. Psychol.*, **46**, 199–210.

LUCHINS, A. S. (1947). Proposed Methods for Studying Degrees of Rigidity in Behavior. *J. Person.*, **15**, 242–246.

MANGAN, G. F. (1959). A Factorial Study of Speed, Power and Related Temperament Variables. *Brit. J. Educ. Psychol.*, **29**, 144–154.

McINTOSH, D. M. (1944). The Effect of Practice in Intelligence Test Results. *Brit. J. Educ. Psychol.*, **14**, 44–45.

McMEEKEN, A. M. (1939). *The Intelligence of a Representative Group o* ↕*Scottish Children*. University of London Press.

McNEMAR, Q. (1940). A Critical Examination of the University of Iowa Studies of Environmental Influences upon the I.Q. *Psychol. Bull.*, **37**, 63–92.

McNEMAR, Q. (1940a). Sampling in Psychological Research. *Psychol. Bull.*, **37**, 331–365.

McNEMAR, Q. (1942). *The Revision of the Stanford-Binet Scale*. Boston, Mass.: Houghton Mifflin.

MELLONE, M. A. (1944). *Moray House Picture Intelligence Test No. 1.* University of London Press.

MINISTRY OF EDUCATION (1950). *Reading Ability.* Pamphlet No. 18. H.M.S.O.

MINISTRY OF EDUCATION (1957). *Standards of Reading 1948–1956.* Pamphlet No. 32. H.M.S.O.

MORRISBY, J. R. (1955). *Differential Test Battery.* National Foundation for Educational Research.

MUNDY, L. (1957). Environmental Influence on Intelligence Function as Measured by Intelligence Tests. *Brit. J. Med. Psychol.,* **30,** 194–201.

MUNDY, L. and MAXWELL, A. E. (1958). Assessment of the Feebleminded. *Brit. J. Med. Psychol.,* **31,** 201–210.

NATIONAL FOUNDATION FOR EDUCATIONAL RESEARCH (Various Authors—undated). *Verbal, Non-verbal, English and Arithmetic Tests.* National Foundation for Educational Research in England and Wales.

NATIONAL INSTITUTE OF INDUSTRIAL PSYCHOLOGY (1923). *Group Test 33;* (1939) *Group Test 70/23;* (1948) *Group Test 90.* National Institute of Industrial Psychology.

NEALE, M. D. (1958). *Neale Analysis of Reading Ability.* Macmillan.

NEWMAN, H. H., FREEMAN, F. N. and HOLZINGER, K. J. (1937). *Twins: A Study of Heredity and Environment.* University of Chicago Press.

NISBET, J. D. (1957). Intelligence and Age: Retesting with Twenty-four Years Interval. *Brit. J. Educ. Psychol.,* **27,** 190–198.

NISBET, S. D. (1939). Non-dictated Spelling Tests. *Brit. J. Educ. Psychol.,* **9,** 29–44.

NORRIS, K. E. (1940). *The Three R's and the Adult Worker.* Montreal: McGill University Press.

OAKLEY, C. A. (1935). A New Formboard. *Human Factor,* **9,** 105–108.

PATTERSON, C. H. (1951). *The Wechsler-Bellevue Scales: A Guide to Counselors.* Springfield, Ill.: Thomas.

PEEL, E. A. (1951). A Note on Practice Effect in Intelligence Tests. *Brit. J. Educ. Psychol.,* **21,** 122–125.

PENROSE, L. S. (1938). *A Clinical and Genetic Study of 1280 Cases of Mental Defect.* Med. Res. Counc. Rep., H.M.S.O.

PERCIVAL, T. S. (1951). *A Standardised French Grammar Test.* University of London Press.

*PIAGET, J. (1950). *The Psychology of Intelligence.* Routledge and Kegan Paul.

PILLINER, A. E. G., SUTHERLAND, J. and TAYLOR, E. G. (1960). Zero Error in Moray House 11+ Verbal Reasoning Tests. *Brit. J. Educ. Psychol.,* **30.**

PINTNER, R. and PATERSON, D. G. (1917). *A Scale of Performance Tests.* New York: Appleton-Century.

PORTEUS, S. D. (1952). *The Porteus Maze Test Manual.* Harrap.

RAVEN, J. C. (1938 and 1947). *Progressive Matrices.* H. K. Lewis.

RAVEN, J. C. (1939). The R.E.C.I. Series of Perceptual Tests: An Experimental Survey. *Brit. J. Med. Psychol.,* **18,** 16–34.

RAVEN, J. C. (1943). *Mill Hill and Crichton Vocabulary Scales.* H. K. Lewis.

RICHARDSON, C. A. (1922). *Simplex Group Intelligence Scale.* Harrap.

RICHARDSON, C. A. (1932). *Simplex Junior Intelligence Test.* Harrap.

ROBERTS, J. A. F. (1939). Intelligence and Family Size. *Eugen. Rev.,* **30,** 237–247.

ROBERTS, J. A. F. (1952). Genetics of Mental Deficiency. *Eugen. Rev.*, **44,** 71–83.

ROBERTS, J. A. F. and MELLONE, M. A. (1952). On the Adjustment of Terman-Merrill I.Q.s to Secure Comparability at Different Ages. *Brit. J. Statist. Psychol.*, **5,** 65–80.

ROGERS, C. A. (1953). The Structure of Verbal Fluency. *Brit. J. Psychol.*, **44,** 368–380.

SARASON, S. B. and GLADWIN, T. (1958). Psychological and Cultural Problems in Mental Subnormality. A Review of Research. *Genet. Psychol. Monogr.*, **57,** 3–284.

SARE, G. T. (1951). *Complexity of Gestalt as a Factor in Mental Testing.* M.A. Thesis, University of London Library.

SCHMIDT, B. (1946). Changes in Personal, Social and Intellectual Behavior of Children Originally Classified as Feebleminded. *Psychol. Monogr.*, **60,** No. .5

SCHONELL, F. J. (1932). *Essentials in Teaching and Testing Spelling.* Macmillan.

SCHONELL, F. J. (1942). *Backwardness in the Basic Subjects.* Edinburgh: Oliver and Boyd.

SCHONELL, F. J. (1945). *The Psychology and Teaching of Reading.* Edinburgh: Oliver and Boyd.

SCHONELL, F. J. and ADAMS, R. H. (1940). *Essential Intelligence Test.* Edinburgh: Oliver and Boyd.

*SCHONELL, F. J. and SCHONELL, F. E. (1950). *Diagnostic and Attainment Testing.* Edinburgh: Oliver and Boyd.

SCHONELL, F. J. and SCHONELL, F. E. (1957). *Diagnosis and Remedial Teaching in Arithmetic.* Edinburgh: Oliver and Boyd.

SCOTT, G. C. (1950). Measuring Sudanese Intelligence. *Brit. J. Educ. Psychol.*, **20,** 43–54.

SCOTTISH COUNCIL FOR RESEARCH IN EDUCATION (1949). *The Trend of Scottish Intelligence.* University of London Press.

SEMEONOFF, B. and TRIST, E. L. (1958). *Diagnostic Performance Tests.* Tavistock Publications.

SHIPLEY, W. C. (1940). A Self-administering Scale for Measuring Intellectual Impairment and Deterioration. *J. Psychol.*, **9,** 371–377.

*SHUEY, A. M. (1958). *The Testing of Negro Intelligence.* Holborn Publ. Co.

SHUTTLEWORTH, F. K. (1935). The Nature versus Nurture Problem. *J. Educ. Psychol.*, **26,** 561–578, 655–681.

SIMON, B. (1953). *Intelligence Testing and the Comprehensive School.* Lawrence and Wishart.

SLEIGHT, G. F. (1931). *Sleight Non-verbal Intelligence Test.* Harrap.

SMITH, C. M. (1948). *Mental Testing of Hebridean Children in Gaelic and English.* University of London Press.

SMITH, D. E. (1951). Some Aspects of the Handwriting of School Children in Aberdeen: A Comparison with American Methods. *Durham Res. Rev.*, **2,** 30–32.

SPEARMAN, C. (1927). *The Abilities of Man.* Macmillan.

SUTHERLAND, J. (1952). An Investigation into the Prognostic Value of Certain Arithmetic Tests at the Age of Eleven Plus. *Brit. J. Statist. Psychol.*, **5,** 189–196.

TERMAN, L. M. *et al.*, *Genetic Studies of Genius.* (1925) I. *Mental and Physical Traits of a Thousand Gifted Children.* (1926) II. *The Early Mental Traits of Three Hundred Geniuses.* (1930) III. *The Promise of Youth.* (1947) IV. *The Gifted Child Grows Up.* V. *The Gifted Group at Mid-Life.* Stanford, Cal.: Stanford University Press.

TERMAN, L. M. and MERRILL, M. A. (1937). *Measuring Intelligence.* Harrap.

THOMSON, G. H. (1939). *The Factorial Analysis of Human Ability.* University of London Press.

THOMSON, G. H. *et al.*, *Moray House Adult Intelligence Test.* University of London Press.

THOMSON, G. H. and LAWLEY, D. N. (1942). New Norms for Ballard's Reading and Arithmetic Tests for Seven-Year-Olds. *Brit. J. Educ. Psychol.*, **12**, 56–58.

THORNDIKE, E. L. (1922). Practice Effects in Intelligence Tests. *J. Exper. Psychol.*, **5**, 101–107.

THORNDIKE, E. L. *et al.* (1928). *Adult Learning.* New York: Macmillan.

THOULESS, R. H. (1930). *Straight and Crooked Thinking.* Hodder and Stoughton.

TIZARD, J. (1951). The Porteus Maze Test and Intelligence: A Critical Survey. *Brit. J. Educ. Psychol.*, **21**, 172–185.

TOMLINSON, T. P. (1953). *The Tomlinson Junior School Test.* University of London Press.

TRAVERS, R. W. M. (1938). The Elimination of the Influence of Repetition on the Score of a Psychological Test. *Annals Eugen.*, **8**, 303–318.

TUDDENHAM, R. D. (1948). Soldier Intelligence in World Wars I and II. *Amer. Psychologist*, **3**, 54–56.

VALENTINE, C. W. (1948). *Intelligence Tests for Children* (3rd edit.). Methuen.

VALENTINE, C. W. (1954). *Reasoning Tests.* Edinburgh: Oliver and Boyd.

VERNON, P. E. (1937). A Study of the Norms and Validity of Certain Mental Tests at a Child Guidance Clinic. *Brit. J. Educ. Psychol.*, **7**, 72–88, 115–137.

VERNON, P. E. (1938). *The Standardization of a Graded Word Reading Test.* University of London Press.

VERNON, P. E. (1948). Indices of Item Consistency and Validity. *Brit. J. Statist. Psychol.*, **1**, 152–166.

VERNON, P. E. (1949). *Graded Arithmetic Mathematics Test.* University of London Press.

VERNON, P. E. (1950). *The Structure of Human Abilities.* Methuen.

VERNON, P. E. (1951). Recent Investigations of Intelligence and its Measurement. *Eugen. Rev.*, **43**, 125–137.

VERNON, P. E. (1953). *Personality Tests and Assessments.* Methuen.

VERNON, P. E. (1954). Practice and Coaching Effects in Intelligence Tests. *Educ. Forum*, **8**, 269–280.

VERNON, P. E. (1956). *The Measurement of Abilities* (2nd edit.). University of London Press.

VERNON, P. E. (ed.) (1957). *Secondary School Selection.* Methuen.

VERNON, P. E. (1957a). Intelligence and Intellectual Stimulation during Adolescence. *Indian Psychol. Bull.*, **2**, 1–6.

VERNON, P. E. (1958). *Educational Testing and Test-Form Factors.* Princeton, New Jersey: Educational Testing Service, RB-58-3.

VERNON, P. E. and PARRY, J. B. (1949). *Personnel Selection in the British Forces.* University of London Press.

WAKELAM, B. B. (1944). The Application of a New Intelligence Test in an Infant School and the Prediction of Backwardness. *Brit. J. Educ. Psychol.*, **14**, 242–250.

WALLIN, J. E. W. (1956). *Mental Defect.* Brandon, Vt.: Journal of Clinical Psychology.

WALTON, R. D. (1948). *Geometry Attainment Test.* University of London Press.

WARBURTON, F. W. (1952). *The Selection of University Students.* Manchester University Press.

WATSON, G. B. and GLASER, E. M. (1942). *Watson-Glaser Critical Thinking Appraisal.* Yonkers-on-Hudson, N.Y.: World Book Co.

★WATTS, A. F. (1944). *The Language and Mental Development of Children.* Harrap.

WATTS, A. F. (1958). *Sentence Reading Test.* National Foundation for Educational Research.

WATTS, A. F. and SLATER, P. (1950). *The Allocation of Primary School Leavers to Courses of Secondary Education.* Newnes.

WATTS, A. F. et al. (1952). *Secondary School Entrance Examinations.* Newnes.

★WECHSLER, D. (1939). *Measurement of Adult Intelligence.* Baltimore, Md.: Williams and Wilkins.

WELFORD, A. T. (1958). *Ageing and Human Skill.* Oxford University Press.

WILSON, R. C., GUILFORD, J. P. et al. (1954). A Factor-Analytic Study of Creative-Thinking Abilities. *Psychometr.*, **19**, 297–311.

WISEMAN, S. *Manchester General Ability Test (Senior I).* University of London Press.

YATES, A. and PIDGEON, D. A. (1957). *Admission to Grammar Schools.* Newnes.

YOAKUM, C. S. and YERKES, R. M. (1920). *Mental Tests in the American Army.* Sidgwick and Jackson.

INDEX

Technical terms are defined on the pages indicated below in heavy type

schemata, **32–4,** 35, 38, 39, 41–2
Schmidt, B., 151, 157, 167, 198
Schonell, F. J., 101, 120, 198
  attainment tests, 20, 93–4, 95, 96,
  98, 100–1, 198
Schonell and Adams Essential
  Intelligence Test, 89, 198
school organisation and intelligence,
  186–8
scientific ability, 90, 179, 184
scoring of tests, 44–5
  mechanical, 26
Scott, G. C., 177, 198
Scottish Council for Research in
  Education, 21, 53, 55, 110, 132–3,
  160–1, 198
Scottish Mental Surveys, 21, 133, 142,
  160–1
secondary school selection, 12, 16, 18,
  21, 45, 50, 89, 92, 93, 96, 98–100,
  111, 115–16, 118, 122–4, 126–7,
  131, 134–7, 148, 154, 165, 170n,
  181, 182, 184, 185–8, 190
Selection Ratio, **124**
Semeonoff, B., 68, 198
sex differences, 77, 129, 134, 164,
  170–1
Shipley, W. C., 86, 198
Shuey, A., 175, 198
Shuttleworth, F. K., 146, 198
Similarities tests, 14, 58, 59, 86, 172
Simon, B., 109n, 198
Simplex Junior, 20, 89
Simplex test, 20
Skeels, H. M., 149–50
Skodak, M., 149–50
Sleight Non-verbal Intelligence Test,
  88–9, 198
Smith, C. M., 176, 198
Smith, D. E., 100, 198
social intelligence, 88
socio-economic class, 18, 19, 34, 40–1,
  109, 115, 138, 141–5, 146, 149–50,
  155, 157–9, 167, 173
spatial ability, 22–4, 55, 66–7, 85,
  171, 175, 179–80, 190,
Spearman, C., 12–14, 17, 21–4, 30,
  31, 41, 48, 76, 81, 178, 198

speed factor in intelligence tests, 18,
  24, 76, 181–2
spelling, 163–4
  tests, 15, 16, 44, 46, 95, 97–8, 179
Spencer, Herbert, 27–8
standard deviation, 50, **105,** 106–8
  129
standard error, **113,** 123
standard scores, **50–1,** 105, 108, 111
standardisation, 15, 44–5, **48–51,** 55,
  115–16
Stanford-Binet Scale, 10–11, 17, 19,
  20, 44–5, 60, 105–7, 110, 128,
  133–4, 140, 146–7, 151, 161, 175
Star Picture test, 66
Stern, W., 11
streaming, 185–8
Substitution test (Wechsler), 59, 60,
  82, 172
Summerfield, A., 185, 196
Sutherland, J., 182, 198

Teacher and Class test, 66
Terman, L. M., 10–11, 17, 29, 48, 76,
  114, 138, 142, 150, 168–70, 191,
  199
Terman-Merrill test, 20, 42, 45, **52–6,**
  57, 59, 60, 61, 62, 64, 67, 104,
  110, 117, 118, 119–20, 129, 155n,
  161, 166, 179, 181, 182, 199
test battery, **75,** 130
tests, administration of, 44–5, 52,
  62–3, 73–4, 75, 135–7, 177
  construction of, 14, 45–6, 75–6,
  109n, 111, 177
thinking, development of, 34–9, 41–2
Thomson, G. H., 18–19, 22, 41, 76,
  95, 141–2, 159, 195, 199
Thorndike, E. L., 15, 17, 25, 30, 48,
  88, 155–6, 173, 193, 199
Thouless, R. H., 36–7, 199
Thurstone, L. L., 22, 31, 40, 102, 178
Tizard, J., 69, 199
Tomlinson Junior School Test, 88,
  199
Translation tests, 82
Travers, J. M. W., 135n, 199
Trist, E. L., 68, 198